THE TRIAD OF STOICISM

The Ancient Teachings of Marcus Aurelius, Seneca & Epictetus To Cultivate Inner Peace

CHOYO GOMEX

ISBN:
9798348151119 (Paperback)
9798348152123 (Hardcover)

Disclaimer Notice:

Please note that the information in this document is for educational and entertainment purposes only. All efforts have been made to present accurate, up-to-date, reliable, and complete information. No warranties of any kind are declared or implied. Readers acknowledge that the author is not engaged in the rendering of legal, financial, medical, or professional advice. The content in this book has been derived from various sources. Please consult a licensed professional before attempting any techniques outlined in this book.

By reading this document, the reader agrees that the author is under no circumstances responsible for any direct or indirect losses incurred as a result of using the information contained within it, including, but not limited to, errors, omissions, or inaccuracies.

Table of Contents

Introduction

Being good is the same as being a philosopher. If you obey your father, you will follow a man's will; if you choose the philosopher's life, the will of the universe.

It is plain, therefore, that your duty lies in the pursuit of philosophy. -Gaius Musonious Rufus.

Life is a wild ride, a roller coaster of highs and lows. One moment, you're soaring at the peak of joy, and the next, you're plummeting into the depths of despair. It's a journey full of twists and turns, with no map or guide to show you the way. The mystery lies in the sheer unpredictability of life's events.

Amidst all these whirlwinds of events, mystery, and unpredictability, there is always a way. It is not a way out but rather a way through life, and it comes in the form of Stoicism. You can not compete with life in being unpredictable, chaotic, or mysterious. It has all that covered. The greatest thing you can do is to find your way through it. Paddle through the storms that the sea of life presents like a duck in still water. Be a Stoic.

Embrace Stoicism, and you'll find yourself in control, no longer at the mercy of life's whims. Just look at the great men who have walked this path before you. They were not victims of circumstance but masters of their destiny. Why should you be any different?

Stoicism is a proven and true pragmatic philosophy, and whoever chooses the Stoic path wins either way, in good times or bad times. One of the most remarkable men to have been shaped by Stoic philosophy is Marcus Gaius Ceaser, often referred to as one of the last true Roman leaders. The man paddled through the storms of life with honor and victory. You can, too.

Stoic philosophy as a way of life is not short of stories of great men who stood tall in difficult times. Their dedication to Stoicism shaped them into men of great stature and repute. One such man is Gaius Musonious Rufus. He lived and thrived at a time when those who embraced Stoicism were outlawed in Rome. He was not obliged to the whims of the rulers. He adhered to the will of the universe and the principles of Stoic philosophy. He practiced Stoicism with both heart and mind.

At such a difficult time, this great Roman not only stayed in Rome and practiced his philosophy with courage, but he also thought it. Neither shame nor fear stopped him from doing what he believed was the universe's will. One of his notable students was Epictetus, who was known for his letters.

The exciting thing about Epictetus is that he presents the possibility of what is often thought impossible to the world. He rose from slave to ruler. Being a dedicated Stoic, Epictetus could withstand unimaginable hardships as a slave in Rome. Ultimately, the discipline of being a Stoic saw him rise through the ranks.

This is not to forget the great Roman Emperor Marcus Aurelius. He will be forever cherished as the man who blessed the world with the excellent text 'Meditations.' That is beside the point. Marcus Aurelius was one of the greatest leaders to come out of and rule Rome. He is remembered for his fairness and peaceful reign. During his tenure, Rome developed considerably and gained more glory. Being a Stoic, he led with courage and wisdom.

Marcus Aurelius' story is one of the most interesting because the man held the most powerful position in the world then. Rome was the greatest empire at the time, and he was at the helm of it. If he willed something, it had to be done. However, despite such great power, Marcus demonstrated a great sense of restraint and discipline. He adhered to Stoic principles and gave Rome its best leadership. In the process, he set an excellent example for other leaders of powerful world nations. Former American president Bill Clinton is known to admire Marcus significantly and was inspired by Marcus' meditations.

Of course, we are not forgetting the remarkable story of Cato, who is considered by many as the last man standing when the Roman Republic fell. He was as eloquent as he was straightforward. He was ever on the side of the people, and when Julius Caesar was not so friendly to the people of Rome, Cato was there to oppose his archaic methods of ruling. Even on the days that Julius Caesar would shelter in his eloquence and often try to use it to convince the people, Cato would, in matching eloquence, call him out. He is a man who embodied Stoic philosophy and wore it like his armor.

Stoic philosophy as a way of life is not short of stories of greatness and endurance, honor, and courage. It would not be wrong to say Stoicism made great men who then made the philosophy even more admirable. They did not fail as the ambassadors of the great philosophy they wholeheartedly embraced.

This book provides a detailed account of the benefits of Stoicism. It is an eye-opener to the Stoic way and the importance of Stoicism as a philosophy and a practical guide to embracing Stoicism as a way of life.

After reading this book, you'll notice two significant improvements in your life. First, embracing Stoicism's philosophy will simplify your life. When you follow its clear principles, making decisions and facing daily challenges becomes easier. Second, your life will not just change--it will get better. You'll find yourself enjoying every day more and feeling more relaxed and confident.

Chapter 1

Foundations of Ancient Stoic Wisdom

He suffers more than necessary, who suffers before it is necessary. -Seneca

Stoicism is a school of ancient philosophical thought, with its origins stemming from Athens, which is modern-day Cyprus, and its earliest proponent being Zeno of Citium. Zeno is also said to have been immensely influenced by the teachings of Socrates. In Zeno's argument, Logos, or universal reason, is the greatest aspect of living a good and satisfying life. In his teachings, he defined Stoic philosophy as a way of life where logic is superior to impulse and emotion as far as taking action is concerned.

Zeno taught stoicism around 300 BCE, during the Hellenistic period. He was the very first propounder and founder of Stoicism as a practice. Zeno used to gather his followers for public teachings. The teachings of Stoicism did not become transient simply because Zeno departed this life; his followers took over the spread of the Stoic gospel during the Hellenistic period. The most active of his immediate followers during that period were Cleanthes and Chrysipus.

Cleanthes and Chrysipus brought notoriety to Stoicism, which led to the discovery of philosophy in Rome. There, the highborn and aspiring leaders received it with open arms. It became a distinguishing way of life and a practical philosophy.

In Rome, the Stoic philosophy's most notable proponents were Seneca, a philosopher and statesman well known for his reasonable leadership style and impeccable performance as the advisor to Emperor Nero. Then they had Epictetus, a former slave who could never let the chains hold him down forever, and eventually, he rose to become a great philosopher. There is no doubt that Rome was a fertile ground for Stoicism to thrive--it further found a proponent in Marcus

Aurelius, the great Roman emperor, also known as Rome's last true emperor and philosopher king.

Stoicism gained notoriety worldwide because of Marcus Aurelius's status as emperor and benevolent leader. Marcus Aurelius's life clearly shows that stoicism is a virtue-based philosophy. It teaches that virtue triumphs over all other ways.

What Stoicism is not

To begin with, there is a difference between upper- and lower-case Stoicism. Upper-case Stoicism is often used to refer to the ancient Greek philosophy practiced by Epictetus. On the other hand, lower-case stoicism refers to a common practice by people who want to suppress their emotions. The lack of this distinction always brings confusion, especially for individuals who cannot differentiate between the two kinds.

There have been misconceptions and discussions surrounding Stoicism and those who practice it as a way of life. Sometimes, it has been misinterpreted by many people worldwide to be some way of life that turns a person cold and non-caring simply because Stoicism advocates for you to stay with the cause no matter the circumstances. It teaches you to live in the moment and not overly worry about future problems.

Often, people refer to Stoics as people who cut themselves off from others and thrive in isolation. However, that is not the case. Stoics thrive in living their lives fully in society with others. The only difference is that Stoics live in moderation. They apply logic in most circumstances and do not submit to their emotions when making decisions. Some of the greatest Stoics lived in full public glamour and fully engaged in society's activities. Those who lived a Stoic life, like Marcus Aurelius, were the greatest contributors to the advancement of their societies.

There is also some discussion about Stoicism as a humorless approach to life, which is not valid. Most of the renowned Stoics had a good sense of humor. It can even be argued that great Stoics of the past preferred good humor instead of anger. Humor takes the place of anger, and it moderates anger. Stoicism is all about the moderation of emotions like anger, which has far more negative than positive consequences.

Another misinterpretation occurs when people start thinking of Stoicism as a way of life that ignores emotions. That is a wrong approach to Stoicism that sometimes stems from a wrong interpretation of Stoic scripts like Marcus Aurelius' Meditations. At some point, you may hear statements where Marcus gives testimony to shutting out emotions in certain instances. However, those emotions were not shut out.

The Four Cardinal Virtues

The main aim of Stoic philosophy is to lead one into living and establishing a Eudaemonic life, that is, a flourishing life and satisfaction. To nurture this path or accomplish this way of life, the very fabric of Stoic philosophy is embedded in four principles, which could be said to be the foundational ethos of Stoicism. The four cardinal values are courage, temperance, justice, and wisdom.

Without these four cardinal virtues, Stoicism would probably not be an excellent way to lead your life. The four cardinal principles give flesh to its bones and make it worthy of practice. They have been given a closer look as follows:

• Courage

Courage stands tall among the cardinal principles of Stoicism. Before we understand it as a Stoic cardinal principle, let us look at it in general. Can courage be understated? Of course not. Widely acclaimed tales have been told about courageous men and women worldwide. Individuals who have showcased great fits of courage often end up in the great books of history.

What is courage? In simple terms, courage is the ability to take action in situations in which you would generally feel fear. That significant step you take in the face of adversity, or that random act you do when everyone else is simply afraid to, is a demonstration of courage.

In the context of Stoicism, courage lays the foundation for the other virtues. In Stoic philosophy, courage does not mean the absence of fear, not at all. It is the ability to take action despite the existence of fear. This means that Stoicism does not implore you to close out your fear. Fear is okay. It is a regular thing. However, stoicism shows you that you can still act even when you are in fear, which is what courage is.

The courage demonstrated and advocated for in Stoicism tells you to stand firm in adversity. You should in no way abandon your principles and virtues because of the challenges you are facing. Taking action, even with the existence of those challenges, is the very essence of courage.

• Temperance

Temperance is a cardinal principle of Stoic philosophy. It means controlling or moderately eating to the essentials. It requires self-control and moderation in one's urge for material things and other desires.

After all, "You ask what the proper limit to a person's wealth is. First, having what is essential, and second, having what is enough." Temperance was taught and embraced in all realms of Stoic philosophy. All the renowned proponents of Stoicism had something special to say about it. Aristotle called it a 'golden mean,' and Epictetus called it "curb your desire.'

The essence of Temperance is to help you find satisfaction in what you have or possess. Wanting more when you have what is essential to your needs is fueled by greed. Stoicism, a philosophy founded on the ethos of the highest good, does not recognize greed.

When you practice temperance and are content with what you have, you will live a life of fulfillment. Wanting more means constant worry about tomorrow or even about getting more.

• Wisdom

Philosophy can be interpreted as a love for wisdom. Wisdom is one of Stoicism's crucial principles, and it allows one to discern between good and evil.

Wisdom is demonstrated in words and has to be embedded in your actions. It will enable you to navigate life's challenges with clarity, resilience, and ethical integrity. In the end, inner tranquility and contentment are expected to be achieved.

Stoicism teaches the practice of applying logos in all instances. That means wisdom informs action. "Between stimulus and response, there is a space. In that space, it is our power to choose our response."

• Justice

Marcus Aurelius and Cicero agreed that wisdom crowns all the other principles of Stoic philosophy. They made it clear that the essence of those other principles was to supplement the principle of justice.

Courage, temperance, and wisdom are all principles centered on the individual or the self. Justice, on the other hand, is based on the greater good. It serves others above all. That makes it the towering principle of Stoicism, representing all the good that practicing Stoicism can achieve.

Justice requires that you do no harm to others and act in good faith. Engage in acts that alleviate society's troubles as opposed to actions that are malice and contribute to societal upheavals.

Be fair, kind, considerate, and truthful. Those principles are embedded in the fabric as the pillar principles of Stoicism.

Eudaemonia and The Triangle of Happiness

The Stoic Eudaemonia and Triangle of Happiness are based on accepting that we can control only so much. In the Eudaemonic approach, happiness is based on pleasing your inner 'daemon,' which refers to your highest self. This indicates that the path to happiness is by pleasing your highest self.

The Stoic Eudaemonia is founded on three principles that act as guiding pillars in its pursuit. The first is to live with Arete. This means that you live in the here and now. It does not end there; it also requires that as you live in the here and now, you live in your best version. That the version of yourself that is living in the moment has to be your best version. To achieve that, you must always ensure that your actions align with your deep values.

Secondly, focus on what you can control. This is based on the fact that everything else is really beyond our control. You cannot control what people think or say about you. They can say and think what they want, and you can do nothing about it. Stoicism teaches you to disregard the opinions that others have about you and embrace your true self without worry or fear. Let those remain their opinions and not a control arm of your life.

It does not end there; it also extends to other naturally occurring events you cannot control as a mortal being. The things generally considered are the will of the gods, God, or the Universe. For example, do you not know what tomorrow will look like? Stoicism implores you to live in the moment and embrace the present fully.

The Nine Core Stoic Beliefs

Like any other critical philosophy of life, Stoicism has a particular set of beliefs apart from having cardinal principles. This set of beliefs is in-depth and aims to guide you to live an entire Stoic life and appreciate the true essence of Stoic philosophy. The nine core Stoic beliefs are as follows:

• Living according to nature.

Zeno of Citium, the first proponent of Stoicism, taught the importance of living in harmony with nature. His teachings indicated that in Stoicism, God was not above nature but somewhat interdependent with nature. In Stoic philosophy, God and nature are on a similar level. Zeno taught that life becomes smoother the moment it is harmonized with nature. He believed that everyone had an inner 'daemon ' or a genius inside that was aligned with our true purposes in the universe. By living harmoniously with nature, you are fulfilling your purpose.

• A happy life can only be found in the pursuit of virtue.

Stoicism is based on the advancement of virtue to find happiness. The philosophy impresses upon the belief that happiness can only be achieved by attaining the highest good. The highest good is a product of living a highly virtuous life.

• You have no control over external events.

Living a Stoic life indicates that you understand that you have no control over things beyond you. People will have opinions about you and formulate a perception of you that they will often use to judge or attack you. However, you are aware that you cannot control people's opinions.

• Utilization of inner resources.

Stoicism operates on the notion that we are each born with a particular set of inner resources to help us navigate the unpredictable journey of life. It emphasizes that all we require is within us, and we only need to tap into our inner selves and embrace those resources within us. In Epictetus' account, those resources include our reason, our power of choice, and the various moral preconceptions. He contended that with these resources, we have every guideline to tackle life rationally and live in harmony with nature and the divine.

• Elimination of toxic emotions.

Most great Stoics dwelled on eliminating toxic emotions because they understood their impact on people's lives. Toxic emotions can lead to failure in one's role within society. Some of what the Stoics highlighted as toxic emotions include anger, fear, and sometimes hope. Putting up hope as a toxic emotion sounds a bit over the top.

The reason why hope was included in the list is that hope is mainly based on expectations of the future. When those expectations are not met, they bring with them immense frustration. Stoicism advocates and emphasizes living in the present. Everything happens in the present, and future events are only a culmination of the events and activities of the present. If you focus on the present, you won't have expectations about the future, saving you a lot of frustration. Living in the present is the epitome of human perfection.

As for the emotion of anger, Seneca pointed out that anger does more harm and damage than it does good. What importance does such an emotion have in one's life when all it achieves is to retrogress your behavior? However, it is essential to note that Stoicism does not advocate suppressing emotions; it instead advocates embracing logic and applying rationale.

Stoicism's teachings about fear indicate that it exists because of worry. Worry results from caring too much about things you cannot control. Fear and worry make you suffer twice for the same thing.

• The rational self.

The rational self is a core belief in Stoicism that stresses taking responsibility for one's actions. It requires not blaming anyone else but oneself and being committed to one's true self.

Zeno of Citium, as the original proponent of the Stoic philosophy, emphasized the harmony of nature and the individual. When you are in harmony with nature, you are in harmony with yourself. An individual who is in harmony operates on rationality as opposed to irrationality.

• The Stoic Golden Rule that 'no man is an island.'

Stoicism's golden rule emphasizes the individual's interconnectedness with society. As an individual, you owe a specific duty to society. The whole point of the golden rule is to emphasize the idea that we all need each other. As such, we need to collaborate and cooperate to exist in harmony. This is our role and duty in society.

• Personal development.

The common good is a concept often impressed upon all through the teachings of great Stoics ranging from Seneca to Marcus Aurelius. When working for the common good, we are also constantly improving ourselves to facilitate the achievement of the common good. This has been emphasized in the other Stoic beliefs, which are our duty to society. It is a call upon us to be each other's keeper.

• Progress and consistency

Stoics have often explained living, or rather life, as the art of continuous progress.

In Stoicism, life is not about perfectionism but rather about improvement.

Even though you might never get precisely where you want to be, you would have made tremendous progress, which is the equivalent of a good life in Stoicism.

A good life is progressive as opposed to retrogressive. In embracing the Stoic way of life, you are embracing a way of life that will instill into your life teachings that can only propel you forward and nothing less.

These are the nine core Stoic beliefs that make Stoicism an exciting way of life. These core beliefs help remove the confusion often brought along by the proponents of small-case stoicism, which is fundamentally distinct from Stoic philosophy.

Cultivating a Stoic Mindset

To fully embrace Stoicism, incorporate it into your life, and get deep into Stoicism, you must cultivate a Stoic mindset. Stoic leaders like Marcus Aurelius emphasize the role the mind plays in one's life and that if you master your mind, you can quickly master life.

How, then, do you develop a Stoic mindset?

The beauty of Stoicism is that it gives you leeway to start from the easiest of practices as you go deeper into the philosophy. The best way to develop a Stoic mindset is to observe and practice the four core principles of Stoicism in your life. As stated earlier, the core principles of stoicism are wisdom, courage, temperance, and justice. In every step you take or every decision you are bound to take, ensure that you have considered all the core principles of stoicism to the best degree possible. This way, you gradually develop a Stoic mindset and settle into Stoicism as a way of life.

Journaling and Practicing Self-Reflection

Journaling has become a fundamental process in the growth and development of a Stoic. Without journaling, Marcus Aurelius would not have given the world the marvelous " Meditations " text. Not only does journaling help you grow and reflect on areas of improvement as a Stoic, but it also sets you on the path of having a perfect Stoic mindset. As is evident, journaling is a routine that turns into a habit. Habits become a lifestyle in one way or another.

Journaling for a Stoic is a reflective process that requires commitment and the most profound sense of honesty with oneself. Stoic journaling can be implemented as follows:

• **Journaling in preparation for the day.**

In the morning, before you start your day, take journaling as your reflective exercise to set the pace for the rest of your day. The Stoic dichotomy of control reminds us that when things go wrong, the best way to react is without anger. On any given day, something is bound to go wrong; that is just life's way. What matters is how you react to whatever goes wrong. Marcus Aurelius habitually reminded himself of the people he would meet during the day. He started his day on the understanding that the people he would encounter might be unpleasant, unfriendly, and unnecessarily rude.

Like Aurelius, it is essential that as you do your reflective journaling each morning, you note down the nature of the people that you will encounter during the day. Then, write it down as a reminder that you cannot let them into whatever negativity they may bring. Remember in reflective writing that you will not let any adverse reaction be a part of your day's interaction. This is a great way to start a day with tranquility.

As a part of your morning journaling as a Stoic, write down all the things you anticipate could go wrong during the day. This is a way to alert your mind and keep yourself aware that things could go wrong, and you should be prepared for a calm reaction to all of them.

• Night journaling to reflect on the happenings of the day.

The habit of night journaling did not start today. The great Stoic Seneca is widely known for this very habit. Seneca writes that every night after his wife had fallen asleep, he would sit down to reflect on his day. This helped him know what he might have done wrong and reminded himself that he should not do them again.

You are at liberty to embrace this habit of night journaling. Each night before you settle to sleep, have a reflective conversation with yourself. Write down the activities of the day. Give yourself a tap on the shoulder for all that you did well. For everything you did wrong, remind yourself never to do it again. This fosters immense growth and progress in a Stoic. It keeps your mindset Stoic. You keep improving each day.

• Negative visualization.

Negative visualization is a form of fear setting. In this Stoic exercise, you must visualize everything bound to go wrong. Imagine yourself in that negative situation.

It is like creating a mental simulation of anticipated challenges and negative instances in one's life.

Unlike the other Stoic journaling methods, the fear setting is not a daily exercise. However, it is an exercise you can engage in when anticipating a particular adverse event.

The following are the steps that you can take to make the exercise effective:

The first step is to write down what you are unsure about. This can be anything; there are no limitations.

The second step is to write down the worst that could happen.

The third step is to write down your action in the worst-case scenario. That is, if the worst that you thought could happen happens, what will you do?

The final step is to write down what the best-case scenario could be.

Even though the fear setting, and negative visualization are a bit difficult as Stoic exercises and Stoic journaling exercises, respectively, they play a critical role in helping you take that much-required leap of faith. They also help you mitigate any adverse reaction or emotion that the negative outcome may necessitate.

• **Gratitude journaling.**

This is arguably the most beautiful part of Stoic journaling. You get to reflect on the things that went exactly how they were supposed to and on what could have gone wrong but did not. Gratitude journaling nurtures the spirit of appreciation and gratitude in a Stoic.

Mindfulness and its Benefits

Mindfulness permeates awareness of oneself and the presence of the mind. It trains you to be fully aware of your life and your surroundings. The essence of mindfulness is to nurture compassion, tolerance, and problem-solving. In Stoicism, mindfulness is more of a state of being than a practiced habit.

Mindfulness is a cognitive presence that fosters informed action. It fosters a mindset of being fully immersed in life and its happenings. It improves focus and reduces emotional reactions, mental flexibility, and satisfactory relationships. Mindfulness can be practiced through meditation, self-reflection, and, most importantly, avoiding judgment.

Kindness

Kindness is a critical Stoic trait and a practice often emphasized in Stoic teachings. There are two ways to practice kindness: being kind to yourself and others.

Being kind to others is engraved in the fabric of Stoic philosophy. The philosophy emphasizes the duty that Stoics owe to society, and being kind to others is one way of fulfilling that duty.

Some of the ways a stoic can be kind to others are by complimenting others, participating in uplifting activities, providing guidance, and being a good listener whenever necessary.

Being an Eternal Student

Learning is an endless process. Stoicism advocates for lifelong learning; the most competent human beings keep learning, improving, and growing. There is always something new to learn each moment and each day. Stoicism promotes lifelong learning, which is essential for personal development. Keep learning, and never stop.

Practice Gratitude

Gratitude fosters a positive attitude and approach to life. It enables you to appreciate the good things that have happened in your life. You learn to appreciate the good times and turn the bad ones into opportunities through gratitude. A soul filled with gratitude often looks forward to making positives out of negatives, and with such an attitude, even obstacles can become opportunities.

The next chapter covers the life history of the great Stoic Seneca. It goes deeper into his life and brings to you the various lessons that the tremendous Stoic intended to convey through his practice of Stoicism. Seneca went down in history as a remarkable figure and a worthy proponent of Stoic philosophy, the chapter sheds light on his immense contribution to the development and spread of Stoicism.

Chapter 2

Philosopher, Politician, and Playwright

A look Into Seneca's Practical Teaching

Begin at once to live and count each separate day as a separate life. -Seneca

Lucius Annaeus Seneca was born around 4 BC and lived until 65 AD.

His life was a cocktail of philosophy, adventure, and wealth. The man lived the Stoic way with a touch of wild creativity, wit, class, and adventure that eventually caused people to wonder if he was a genuine Stoic. He made leading a Stoic life look easy.

Seneca was the son of Seneca the Elder. At a young age, Lucius Annaeus Seneca, "the Stoic," was sent to Rome to study philosophy. In Rome, Seneca studied a blend of Stoic and Pythagorean philosophy.

Due to Seneca's extensive knowledge of the Law, philosophy, and politics, he served as consul among the emperor Claudius. At around 40AD, Emperor Claudius and Seneca had a fallout, and Seneca was thrown into exile. He was accused of committing adultery with Julia Livilla, the emperor's niece. After some time, the mother of future emperor Nero and wife to Claudius, pleaded for the release of Seneca so that he could return and perform the role of tutor to the future emperor.

This was a nice turn of events for Seneca the Stoic. as it led to his release back to the everyday world where he would thrive and philosophize. Seneca performed the role of tutor to young Nero, who became emperor, the most notorious of them all-- so much so that it even raised questions about Seneca's character. The reign of young Nero as emperor saw Seneca's wealth rise.

Seneca's challenging life led him to embrace Stoicism fully. He adopted it as his personal philosophy and integrated ideas from other philosophical traditions. Seneca practiced what he preached, writing extensively about philosophy, and living according to his teachings. He became a prominent advocate for Stoicism, teaching and delivering public lectures in Rome's famous halls.

Seneca's life blended Stoic principles with an adventurous spirit, setting him apart from other philosophers. He actively pursued wealth alongside his philosophical endeavors, partly to counter the prevailing belief that philosophers were only thinkers and couldn't be wealthy.

By amassing wealth, Seneca demonstrated that philosophers could indeed be practical and financially successful.

Seneca's life unfolded tragically. He amassed wealth and gained popularity while serving as a tutor and mentor to Nero, a young man he shaped into a leader. However, his growing influence did not sit well with Nero, who became paranoid and suspected Seneca of plotting against him. Tragically, this suspicion led Nero to order Seneca to take his own life--a fate Seneca had managed to avoid under previous rulers. Ultimately, Seneca's life was ended by the very emperor he had dedicated himself to mentor. A profound tragedy indeed!

The Works of Seneca

A great deal of Seneca's legacy is a wide range of philosophical works, which have made him stand out from other proponents of stoicism. Seneca's works are relatable, wild, adventurous, and as classy as the Stoic himself. Some of Seneca's greatest works will be discussed in depth throughout this chapter.

Epistulae Morales: Letters from a Stoic

Seneca's Letters from a Stoic is an epic collection of one hundred and twenty-four Stoic-themed letters written by Seneca to his friend Lucius, the proctodeum of Rome, during emperor Nero's reign. They had served the emperor together. Sometimes, the letters are called 'Epistulae Morales Ad Luciullius', Latin for 'Moral Letter to Lucillius.' The letters are also widely called 'Moral epistles' or 'Letters from a Stoic.'

The letters were addressed to his friend Lucillius even though it has been agreed upon that Seneca would have been considering a wider audience owing to the nature of the teachings in the letters. They were written near the end of Seneca's life when he learned so much about life. His letters came from a point of experience and practicality of life. He had seen it all and lived through it all, and through his letters, he would guide others to live through it all. Seneca was a true Stoic, and this is richly demonstrated in his works.

Seneca's letters from a Stoic have a wide range of lessons to teach and illustrations from his own life to make the message more straightforward to comprehend. Seneca often started with a salutation and a quote in his first letters. The letters carry many notable lessons, among them contentment, embracing the inner self, the joy of wisdom, living in harmony with nature, virtue, and vice, the importance of time and its shortness, death, friendship, coexistence with others, simple living, travel, peace, grief, and philosophy.

Having experienced much in his life, Seneca was generous with his wisdom, using his experiences to enlighten others. His aim was to help people avoid the mistakes he had made and to share the benefits of his Stoic lifestyle. His letters are rich with wisdom and discernment, each beginning with an inspirational quote that sets the tone for the lessons to follow. Below, we summarize Seneca's letters' key themes and insights.

• On embracing our inner selves.

"Seneca places great emphasis on cultivating the inner self in his Epistulae Morales. He advocates for a profound connection with one's innermost thoughts and feelings as a path to harmony with the broader universe and nature itself. According to Seneca, embracing our inner self involves not just self-awareness but also active disengagement from society's pressures and opinions.

He cautions against the distractions of external validation, which can divert us from our true purpose and personal growth.

Seneca argues that our foremost duty is to foster our own well-being and continuous improvement. This philosophy extends to how we interact with others--suggesting that a strong inner self enables us to face the world with confidence and resilience without succumbing to its judgments or condescension.

By focusing inward, we cultivate virtues that resonate more deeply and create a life that is not only in alignment with Stoic principles but also profoundly satisfying and impactful.

Seneca argued that actual inner growth hinges on recognizing and embracing one's flaws. He contends that these imperfections should not be seen as barriers to personal development; instead, they are integral to the journey of self-improvement. In his teachings, Seneca emphasizes that understanding and accepting our flaws allows us to confront and transform them into strengths. This process is not about achieving perfection but about evolving and enriching our character.

By acknowledging our limitations, we set the stage for genuine growth and a deeper understanding of ourselves, aligning more closely with the Stoic ideal of living a virtuous and fulfilled life.

• On Friendship:

In his "Letters from a Stoic," Seneca talks about the importance of friendship. He teaches that to have good friends, you must first be a good friend to yourself. If you can't enjoy your own company, it's tough to be a true friend to others. By learning to appreciate and support yourself, you reduce the need for approval from others. This self-friendship makes it easier to be content and stable on your own.

A Stoic believes that the key to a fulfilling life doesn't come from outside approval.

Your happiness should start with you treating yourself as your own best friend. When you are good to yourself, making friends with others becomes easier. Even if you don't have many friends around, being your own friend is a valuable source of companionship.

Seneca doesn't suggest befriending ourselves as a means to withdraw from society. Instead, he highlights the importance of engaging in community affairs and policies. However, he warns against the pitfalls of conforming to group thinking. According to Seneca, when you think with the crowd, you lose the chance to express your individuality and contribute your unique perspective to the world. He strongly advises against succumbing to the pressure of group consensus.

• On contentment.

According to Seneca, 'enough' consists of life's essentials: food, water, shelter, and a resilient inner self. He believed these are all a person truly needs to live well. While some philosophical schools might encourage you always to seek more, Stoicism values the principle that having enough is plentiful--and that sometimes, enough is truly all you need.

From his life, Seneca learned that philosophy calls for simple living. You do not need to punish yourself or engage in some penance to get more than you have. As long as you have the essentials of life, then that is a life worth embracing.

We often fear living without our earthly possessions, pricey cars, fancy houses, luxurious homesteads, and more. But Stoicism implores us to ignore that worry and acknowledge that so long as we have the essentials, we need not worry but be content that we have enough.

De Brevitate Vitae **"On the Shortness of Life"**

In De Brevitate Vitae, Seneca emphasizes how short life really is and how little time there is to live. He looks at time as the greatest commodity we have and yet the one we have no control over. Time runs out when it does, and whether you agree with it or not does not matter. He acknowledges that you can never live too long, and life is bound to end at some point.

Seneca envisions philosophy as the only way to make meaning out of life's shortness, and this is because philosophy gives life purpose. Instead of spending the short time we have alive worrying about business and making money, we should embrace philosophy so as to make something out of life before time takes us back into nothingness.

He implores us to examine the causes behind life's quick passing. What consumes us for so long that we overlook our lives passing by? He identified things such as too much ambition and giving to others that you forget to live life in its true meaning as some of the things that impact the quickness of life's passing.

Seneca had finally understood that even if you had the most extended life, it would still pass by without you noticing. He pointed out how people were consumed by the chase of worldly glory, profits, and the need to show off their talents and that by the time they realized what was happening, death had already caught up with them. He contends that as a human being, you should seek things that guide you toward purposeful fulfillment and things that give life meaning.

De Clementia **"On Mercy"**

"De Clementia," which translates to "On Mercy," is a work penned by Seneca to advise the Roman Emperor Nero, to whom he served as a personal advisor. In this treatise, Seneca extols the virtues of mercy, arguing that it is an essential attribute for effective leadership.

Seneca presents mercy as a benevolent act and a strategic tool that reinforces a ruler's authority. By choosing mercy, a leader demonstrates awareness and empathy toward ordinary people's daily struggles and potential misjudgments. This approach humanizes the leader and engenders trust and loyalty among the populace.

Furthermore, Seneca discusses how mercy contributes to a more harmonious society. He suggests that when leaders exhibit forgiveness and understanding, it fosters a sense of unity and consensus between those in power and those they govern. According to Seneca, this bond is crucial for maintaining stability and ensuring that governance is not just about enforcing rules but also about nurturing a community.

In "De Clementia," Seneca elaborates on the idea that true strength in leadership comes from the capacity to be lenient. He argues that mercy can defuse potential conflicts and transform them into opportunities for growth and mutual respect.

By advocating mercy, Seneca provides Nero--and, by extension, all leaders--with a philosophical foundation for ruling with kindness as a form of wise and just governance.

Seneca compares the power of a ruler to that of a god. As a matter of universal truth, gods are generally merciful to their subjects, and this can be seen in the divine providence that we often benefit from, even unknowingly. What Seneca tries to impress in De Clementia is that kings and rulers, as well as any other people in positions of power, are representatives of the gods. As such, they should be as merciful as the gods they represent.

Resonating Quotes from Seneca and Their Meaning

The following are some of Seneca's quotes that would leave you reflecting deeply on Stoicism and probably wanting more of it:

"Life is long if you know how to use it."

Seneca quoted this in his work De Brevitate Vitae (On the Shortness of Life). What Seneca meant by the above quote is that life can pass by quickly when you are consumed in chasing things that are not important. On the other hand, when you live a meaningful and purposeful life, that is a long life regardless of the concept of time.

"A gem cannot be polished without friction, nor a man without trials."

In this profound quote, Seneca captures the essential role of adversity in personal growth. He suggests that challenges and difficult times are not merely obstacles to be endured but opportunities to develop strength and resilience. The analogy of a gem being polished through friction underscores the idea that significant and lasting strength in a person comes from facing and overcoming hardships.

Seneca intimates that resilience is necessary for greatness. Standing firm in the face of challenges allows one to survive and thrive. Life's trials are inevitable, but they should not hinder our progress but enhance our character and capabilities. This perspective is particularly valuable during tough times, offering a way to reconcile with reality and find meaning in our struggles.

By embracing this mindset, we can transform our trials into catalysts for personal improvement and deeper understanding.

"He who has a why to live can bear almost any how."

Though famously articulated by Friedrich Nietzsche, this statement aligns closely with Seneca's Stoic philosophy on the importance of purpose in life. Seneca consistently emphasized the value of having a clear and compelling reason for living rather than merely existing without direction. According to Seneca, possessing a life purpose isn't just motivational; it is a guiding force that helps you navigate life's challenges and obstacles.

When you have a clearly defined purpose, you are equipped to face adversity with resilience. This is because your actions and decisions are anchored by your overarching goals, making it easier to endure hardships and setbacks. Seneca believed that with a strong sense of purpose, individuals can maintain their focus and drive, even under severe stress or during crises, as their purpose provides a reason to persevere and overcome.

Seneca's teachings encourage us to find and hold onto our 'why,' suggesting that it can sustain us through almost any 'how.' This perspective helps to cultivate a stoic resilience, enabling individuals to transform their trials into opportunities for growth and strengthening their commitment to their life's goals.

In his works, Seneca always insisted on having a purpose in life instead of just living plainly. When you have a life purpose, you conquer obstacles because your purpose guides you.

"True happiness is to enjoy the present without anxious dependence upon the future."

Seneca consistently underscored the importance of living in the moment, a fundamental aspect of his Stoic teachings. He believed that true contentment comes from fully engaging with the present rather than being preoccupied with the future. According to Seneca, when individuals focus entirely on the present, they enhance their ability to experience life's pleasures and confront its challenges more effectively.

He warned against the perils of excessive future-oriented thinking, which can lead to anxiety and prevent us from appreciating the current moment. Seneca taught that such worry about the future is futile, as it distracts us from the present opportunities and joys. He argued that by always looking ahead, people often repeat the same mistake they made with the past--neglecting it when it was their present.

Seneca suggested that living in the present is not only a pathway to happiness but also a practice in wisdom. It allows individuals to cultivate gratitude, resilience, and a deeper appreciation for the transitory nature of life. By embracing the present, we avoid the tragedy of missing out on our lives as they unfold, a key reason why Seneca so passionately advocated for this approach.

"The greatest remedy for anger is delay."

Anger comes from emotions rather than logic. Seneca, a proponent and teacher of Stoic philosophy, often emphasized the importance of logic, or, as it was famously referred to, the 'logos.'

This means that instead of taking action when you are angry and influenced by emotions, which will make it impossible to act logically, you should delay the reaction so that when your emotions are down. Rationality is restored, and you can act from a logical point of view.

"We do not dare to do many things because they are difficult; they are difficult because we do not dare to do them."

When he made this argument, which led to this quote, Seneca understood that as human beings, we make a big deal out of things. As such, because of the perception that we create in ourselves that a thing is difficult, you realize it is that perception that makes the thing difficult, but in reality, it is not difficult in the first place.

True to it, most of us suffer from this syndrome as we analyze things, tasks, or even goals and conclude at face value that they are difficult. The reality is different, and when you do something that you perceive as complex, you realize it was probably the easiest thing you have ever done. There is a need to be bold and do things without creating a perception that makes a mountain out of an anthill.

Chapter 3

Seneca's Stoic Serenity

Luck is what happens when preparation meets opportunity. -Seneca

As a Stoic, Seneca advocated for a life that is serene and in harmony with nature. The essence of his teachings and stoic works was to guide people towards living a trouble-free and peaceful life.

Stop Overthinking

Seneca and Stoicism consider overthinking a vice. Stoicism discourages overthinking in all circumstances because it is influenced by emotion, which prevents logic from applicability in such instances. In addition, overthinking does not explicitly bring peace of mind. On the contrary, it brings anxiety and unnecessary expectations.

Seneca on Overthinking

Seneca often noted that our imagination is more likely to bring us suffering than reality. This is an effect of overthinking. Our minds pick one minor issue and make a myriad of issues out of it, and by the time we realize it, we have opened a Pandora's box of thoughts.

Overthinking is a result of anxiety and can also bring forth anxiety. In his Letters of a Stoic, Seneca acknowledges that as a human being, you are bound to face obstacles along the way. However, you have no business worrying and overthinking about them in the present when they are yet to happen.

Fixating on the challenges of the future in the present only makes you suffer the same suffering twice. You suffer in your mind because you think of them before they happen, and then you suffer when the challenges happen. This is one of the reasons why Stoic teachings are anchored on living in the moment--embracing the present and not worrying too much about the future because you do not know much about it.

Seneca also acknowledges that the mind often fashions challenges of its own, even when nothing points to that evil. We are often used to anticipating challenges because we are so accustomed to life's challenges that we feel like life cannot be normal without them. Sometimes, life is smooth, and those challenges are nonexistent. However, the mind finds it too difficult to accept that the challenges might not be there this time and begins overthinking. It starts creating imaginary challenges on behalf of life. Then, before you realize it, you are pulled into a web of worry.

Consequences of Overthinking

Overthinking has been ruled as a vice that brings with it too much worry and has been known to have the following consequences.

• It makes your thought process stall.

When you overthink, you spend too much time fixating on one issue, which might only be a construct of your mind--a figment of your imagination. At that moment, you are fixated on one issue, and your thought process is literally in a loop; therefore, it can be said to be stalling. Overthinking can also damage your imagination and make you less innovative.

• It drops your energy levels.

Any form of thinking requires energy. Overthinking, by nature, takes up most of your energy and, in the process, drops your levels.

• It may cause you sleeping problems.

Overthinking brings on worry and opens a can of worms in your mind. It becomes challenging to muster sleep in a worrisome state.

• It hinders your critical thinking capacity.

When your mind is occupied with worry and fixated on one thing, its ability to think critically is hindered or even taken away during that duration.

How to Overcome Overthinking

Stoicism emphasizes worrying only about things you can control. The truth is that worrying about the things you cannot control will not change anything and will, therefore, not solve your problem.

The following are some ways to assert control of your thoughts and overcome overthinking.

• Practice mindfulness.

Mindfulness brings one's mind back into the present. It helps one clear one's mind and focus on the present.

- Focus on what is within your control.

- Journal your thoughts for clarity and perspective.

- Embrace the practice of gratitude to shift your focus to the positive.

- Practice visualization to eliminate negative thoughts.

Life is Short

In Seneca's teachings on the shortness of life, the great Stoic retaliates that life is short not merely because of the duration of one's days of drawing oxygen. This contention is instead grounded on accurate and meaningful living. It highlights how we spend so much time doing insignificant things to our authentic living, which aligns with the universe and is in harmony with nature.

Seneca on Living in the Present

As a proponent and teacher of Stoicism, Seneca often taught the public the importance of living in the present. To him, the present was everything. In his teachings and works, Seneca often made it clear that the past and the future are no longer in our control and, therefore, we should quit worrying about them because the best they can do is bring harm.

When we dwell on the future too much, we develop expectations, which leads to a lot of pressure to meet those expectations. When we fail to meet them, we open the floodgates of anxiety and frustration, which takes away our ability to take advantage fully. How will you be able to take advantage of the present if your mind and efforts are focused on the future?

Seneca also emphasizes that life is too short, and the more you focus on anything that is not present, the more you become oblivious to it. Because life is too short, you must take advantage of every fleeting moment and handle every passing challenge in the present. The most important of Seneca's reminders is that we should leave the past in the past, and the future should wait for the future. The future and the past should not be the factors that influence your present.

Stoicism, through Seneca's teachings, implores you to keep your focus glued on every second and every moment in the present. There is much to gain from the present, as opposed to the past you have left behind and a future you cannot predict. You might spend too much time worrying about the future only to realize you might not even be a part of that future. This gives you reason enough to live in the present and be entirely focused on it.

How to Stay in the Moment

Seneca intimated that to stay in the moment, one must be able to reject any desires of the future and acknowledge the things that are required to make the present moment as fulfilling as possible. The essence of this line of thought or teaching is that if one clears one's mind off the desires of the future, one will be intrigued by the nuances of the present.

When you find the nuances of the present intriguing, you can find answers to the questions of your current situation. Your curiosity will also be focused on the present, which will help you enjoy each moment. Living in the moment means you can analyze the events and happenings of each moment with a depth of presence and focus.

Staying in the moment brings peace and tranquility. You are fully settled into your life and capable of effectively handling whatever you face in each moment. If you do not face any apparent challenges in the present, each moment becomes an opportunity to thrive, where you will be fully aware of your surroundings and actions.

Exercises to Help with Staying in the Moment and Living the Present

The following are some exercises that will come in handy if you live in the present and utilize each passing moment in a fulfilling way.

• Visualize your goals.

Take the initiative of visualizing your goals each morning. Visualizing your goals makes it easier to live each moment mindfully of them. The more you visualize your goals, the more you can strategize on their fulfillment. Visualization is not only about strategizing the possible path to fulfillment of your goals; it also makes it possible to dissect your goals profoundly and keenly.

• Journal prompts.

Journaling has become the go-to method for settling one's mind whenever one is overwhelmed, overthinking, or anxious. When you practice journaling, it often helps you start your day mindfully.

Fight Your Ego

Ego is the unhealthy and arrogant belief in one's abilities. Unfortunately, we are all guilty of having a certain amount of ego, right? However, ego, no matter how common and usual, often leads down the wrong path, where it is easier to believe you are right even when you are wrong.

Ego shapes you into someone who does not learn or take corrections directed to you politely or even embrace them. If you cannot abandon your ego, you sacrifice your ability to learn, correct, and improve. Life seems unfulfilling when you cannot improve and remain stagnant in one state or position for a long time. Good Stoics fight their egos, and they do not let those egos take over their lives because they aim to live a fulfilling life that is in harmony with nature and the will of the universe.

Seneca on Ego

Seneca and many other proponents of Stoicism emphasized the importance of practicing humility and its benefits: Humility, in a way, protects you from ego. You do not need arrogance to prove a point when you practice humility. A person who embraces humility often does not worry about pitting himself against others and, as such, has no use for ego.

In humility, you learn that ego is not essential and acknowledge that ego can fuel unnecessary expectations. Ego puts you in a position where you constantly need to prove yourself, while humility puts you in a position of contentment, which makes it easier for you to have a fulfilling present.

How to Balance Self-Confidence and Self-Awareness

Often, self-confidence is mistaken for ego, and ego is mistaken for self-confidence. However, the two are in complete contrast.

Stoicism's self-confidence is characterized by courage, wisdom, and self-discipline. You need to have the courage to accept your imperfections and acknowledge that perfection is unattainable. As a Stoic, your focus should be on the things you can control rather than on those you cannot control.

Cultivating humility is another way to strike a balance between self-confidence and self-awareness. You must come to understand that you are part of a world with people with different perspectives and that you cannot monopolize such a world and make it yours and yours alone.

All these people are part of something larger than themselves, and so are you. If you believe that you are a part of something larger than yourself, it can only be fair that you acknowledge others and respect their perspectives and opinions. Life around you should not always be about your way or the highway. Show kindness and compassion and acknowledge when you are wrong. A big part of being humble is appreciating others.

Whenever you are in a room full of people, it also helps you to be the calmest person. This a demonstration of your self-awareness and confidence in yourself. Humble confidence often requires peace and clarity--clarity comes from putting in the work and being highly effective, and peace comes from being aware of who you are and the extent of your abilities.

In addition, to strike a balance between self-confidence and self-awareness, it is important to practice gratitude. Be appreciative of the opportunities that come your way, take them to heart, embrace them, and utilize them to the maximum, keeping in mind that someone else is equally desirous of accessing the same opportunities but cannot.

Balancing self-awareness and self-confidence allows you to navigate life's complexities easily.

Never Be a Slave of Your Wealth

Money and wealth have generally taken center stage in modern-day human life. Sometimes, even the world's richest men are castigated for being too wealthy and are considered selfish and greedy. People pursue education and acquire skills to make money and acquire wealth. Others work solely to make money. However, are money and wealth all there is to life? Here is what Seneca, the great Stoic, had to say about money and wealth:

Seneca on Wealth

Before we delve into Seneca's thoughts on wealth, it is worth noting that Seneca was among the wealthiest men of his time in Rome and one of the richest Stoics. Therefore, his thoughts on wealth are unique and rich in experience. Seneca had a straightforward approach to wealth; he considered it a means to an end, not the end itself. Like in modern times, ancient times required resources for survival.

So many times, Seneca emphasized that virtue and moral uprightness were the greatest forms of wealth. However, he was not blind to the need for material wealth. In his 'Letters of a Stoic", Seneca emphasized that wealth was necessary. He maintained that wealth should be considered a neutral aspect of one's life. What mattered most to him was the process that led to a person acquiring or accumulating wealth.

He looked at wealth from the perspective of it being the byproduct of pursuing a worthy cause. For instance, an individual could be an excellent doctor, healing the sick and discovering cures. That person is committed to solving humanity's problems. In pursuing his purpose, he gets paid for excellence in that pursuit. Therefore, such wealth is neutral; it is not acquired through a selfish desire or greed but rather a by-product of a worthy cause.

36

However, Seneca was often against ill-gained wealth or wealth acquired out of greed, selfishness, and desire. For instance, using the same doctor scenario in the previous paragraph, take the example of a doctor who is entirely in the healing business for money. Such a person could be amenable to compromising their integrity for money. Seneca argued from the perspective that such a person is enslaved by wealth.

You can feel the difference everywhere when wealth is acquired through greed instead of as a byproduct of pursuing a worthy cause. Those who pursue wealth often end up being enslaved by it. Their decisions are often influenced by their desire for more wealth, and therefore, they are likely to cause harm to others in the process of acquiring or trying to acquire wealth.

Ultimately, Seneca concluded that wealth is neither good nor bad but relatively neutral. The debate on whether wealth was good or evil to him was limited to the process of acquiring wealth and the people's attachment to their wealth. He, therefore, encouraged people to practice detachment from material wealth.

How to Cultivate Temperance in an Age of Excess

Temperance is a virtuous practice that requires moderation and self-control in all aspects of life.

Stoic philosophy embraces temperance, and Seneca, in his teaching, emphasized being content with what you have. The essence of teaching and practicing temperance is that it is a virtue that limits or slows down the many evils in society. Temperance seeks to answer the question of whether doing things in excess is necessary. This includes over-accumulating wealth, being overly obsessed with fame, and other desires that lead humanity to be excessive in their doing.

The following are ways you can cultivate temperance in yourself.

• Practice moderation.

This is achievable by finding a balanced approach to life. Eliminate the need to indulge in excess or under-indulge. Let all the things you engage in be balanced.

• Practice self-control.

This is the ability to control your urges, indulgencies, impulses, desires, and emotions. The practice of self-control is the bedrock of temperance and moderation.

• Practice ethical living and wise decision-making.

The practice of ethical living and wise decision-making translates to living according to the existing principles of ethics and making decisions that align with such principles.

Stoicism as a philosophy is anchored in the practice of moderation and self-control.

Mindful Eating

Mindful eating is an exercise that allows you to eat food while engaging all of your senses. It emanates from mindfulness, a form of motivation that enables you to enjoy and make present moments last.

To practice mindful eating, you take a bite of whatever food you eat and savor the moment. Use your sense of smell to smell the food before you even eat. As you take the first bite, let the experience savor; let your senses feel the presence of food and taste every bit of it. Allow your senses to enjoy the taste and fully engage.

The importance of mindfulness is it helps control eating habits that are fueled by anxiety, for example, stress eating as well as rush eating. It can also help with calming your mind. In the end, mindful eating is a form of meditation; the only difference with other forms of meditation is that it involves food.

Anti-Consumerist/Minimalist Journal Prompts and Affirmations

Anti-consumerism is a social, economic ideology that seeks to eliminate the need to be overly intrigued by material possessions. It opposes the prioritization of material wealth and equates happiness to the same. Conversely, minimalism is a philosophy that encourages focus on what is essential and necessary and embraces simplicity.

Therefore, this emphasizes decluttering one's life of unnecessary things that do more harm than good.

Manage your Anger.

Stoicism's philosophy advocates for logic in place of emotions. Stoicism has nothing against emotions; however, it emphasizes that emotions are irrational, no matter how normal they may appear to be. Logic, on the other hand, is the cornerstone of rationality. Anger is one of those emotions that takes away a person's rationality.

Seneca on Anger

Seneca viewed anger as an emotion that attacked everyone without discrimination--the brave, calm, gentle leaders and ordinary men alike. Therefore, the secret did not lie in the lack of anger but rather in the control of it. Seneca defined anger as a binary emotion that could take control subconsciously, and by the time you realize it, you are under its control.

In his teachings, Seneca profoundly addressed the destructive nature of anger. He pointed out that anger often harms us more than the situation or person it is directed towards. This insight into the self-inflicted damage caused by anger is a central theme in Stoic philosophy. Seneca advised that recognizing this harmful impact can be a powerful motivator to manage and mitigate our angry responses.

Seneca suggested that when feelings of anger arise, we should remind ourselves that our emotional reaction may be causing more harm to ourselves than the original issue. By doing so, we shift our focus from the external trigger to the internal turmoil, allowing us to gain perspective and control over our emotions.

He believed that understanding the self-harm caused by anger not only reduces the intensity of our emotional responses but also helps us to prioritize our well-being and peace of mind. This self-awareness encourages us to address problems more constructively, focusing on solutions rather than being consumed by negative emotions.

According to Seneca, mastering anger involves recognizing its futility and transforming our reactions into thoughtful responses that align with our values and goals. This approach alleviates personal distress and enhances our interactions and decision-making, leading to a more harmonious and productive life.

He also taught that it is better to consider a person's character whenever you are angry with someone or if that person has done something that angered you. This distracts you from the specific thing that makes you angry and allows you to focus on the person's positive attributes.

When a person has angered you, it is also essential to understand that the person is also human. In any case, you also have your flaws that you can remind yourself about instead of taking out the anger on the person who may have caused it.

Visualization, breathwork, and journaling are some of the exercises you can do whenever you are angry. All of these are effective techniques in anger management.

The next chapter focuses on the story of Epictetus, the former slave who rose from shackles to a revered Stoic. Like Seneca, Epictetus took up Stoicism as a philosophy and a way of life and spent most of his life practicing and teaching It.

Chapter 4

Epictetus Explored. From Shackles to Sage

Demand not that events should happen as you wish, but wish them to happen as they do, and your life will be serene. - Epictetus

The mentioning of Stoicism without mentioning the story of Epictetus and the role he played in the growth of Stoicism can only be termed a grave injustice. Epictetus' story is a universal inspiration transcending time, geographical location, and societal dispositions. He was as resilient as he was tenacious, and perhaps the most important virtue one can learn from Epictetus is resilience. He embodied the virtue of resilience all through his life.

Epictetus' Stoic Liberation

Epictetus, born in 50AD in Hierapolis, Phrygia (present-day Pamuk Kale, Turkey), rose from humble beginnings to become a renowned sage of Stoicism. Epictetus was born and raised a slave and spent most of his young life serving wealthy Roman citizens as a slave.

Being born into slavery, however, did not extinguish the fire and desire for knowledge that was in him. Epictetus had a passion for knowledge that most people admired. This earned him the respect of his master, Epaphroditus, at a young age. It is his master who then hired a tutor, another great Stoic philosopher, Mussonius Rufus, to nurture and tutor Epictetus in the ways and wisdom of philosophy.

After attending Mussonius Rufus's tutoring sessions, he developed a deep passion for Stoicism. Upon earning his freedom, Epictetus established a Stoic philosophy school in Nicopolis, Greece, where he lectured and taught Stoic philosophy. His lectures attracted citizens and the ruling class in equal measure. His lectures and adherence to a Stoic way of life earned him respect and reverence from great leaders and citizens alike. In light of such dedication, Epictetus rose from a mere slave to one of the most influential people.

He faced many challenges, including being exiled. However, Epictetus remained steadfast in his commitment to Stoicism. He embraced and practiced its teachings, and in the end, that discipline and commitment transformed him from an ordinary man to a man who exuded greatness through his doings, teachings, and lifestyle.

The Works of Epictetus

Epictetus is attributed to two main works: Discourses and Enchiridion. These works, written by his followers, compile his teachings and life.

Discourses

Discourses is a magnificent and enticing manuscript encapsulating the teachings of Epictetus and the conversations he would have with his students. The book 'Discourses' takes a thematic approach as opposed to chapters, and the themes in the book have been summarized below as follows:

Introduction to Stoicism: The book's beginning introduces the reader, or rather, the audience, to Stoic philosophy and Stoic practices. He specifically holds dialogues with his students and discusses the Stoic concept of Eudaemonia and the achievement of a fulfilled life by living virtuously.

The dichotomy of control: Much like Seneca, Epictetus had something to say about control in Discourses. He emphasizes the importance of being true to yourself and the constant need for outward validation from other people. Epictetus makes the argument that worrying about things that are beyond your control is a futile exercise because, in truth, you have no control.

Therefore, worrying about the things you can control is only necessary, such as self-improvement and self-focus. Other people's notions of you are not your responsibility but rather theirs. The moment you start to worry about outside notions or perceptions of yourself, you are taking the power of control from yourself and willingly giving it away to the people with such notions.

Still focusing on the dichotomy of control, Epictetus emphasized our reaction to outside events. Most often, we are bound to react using our emotions to every situation. However, that is something that Epictetus constantly grappled with and taught against. He emphasized the power of our judgments that every time we are angry at something, it is time to question not what we are angry about but rather what our judgment has led us to be angry.

The book Discourses brings out the theme of control and the only instance where Epictetus once referred to his years of slavery. He expressed that he did not spend his life being bitter about the times he led a life of slavery. He rather indicates that his master may have had control of his physical body, but his mind was under his control. He did not harbor feelings of hatred and contempt against his master as that would only mean giving away control of his mind to his master.

Epictetus argued that the important lesson from this theme is that our control of situations lies in our logical response to the conditions instead of our instant reaction to them. For instance, you have the most magnificent house that has taken you time and resources to build and furnish. Then, one night, an arsonist's evil mind leads him to your doorstep as you are in a deep and comfortable slumber. The arsonist lights up your house with all its magnificence.

In this scenario, you could have two reactions; one reaction gives you control, and the other leaves you in worry and constant pestering. The usual response is you start questioning why you? Why was it your hard work that the arsonist had to light up? You come up with so many whys that may plunge you into depression and still not solve your current lack of an abode.

The other reaction is to focus on yourself and not the arsonist's actions; ask yourself what will benefit you. At that point, you know the only choice you have is to rebuild; that is the only thing in your control.

Endurance and resilience: Epictetus' story is a marvelous testimony of endurance and resilience. He is a man who did not let circumstances define him. He was born into slavery and grew up as a slave, but deep down, he knew he had to pursue education and acquire more knowledge. He saw and envisioned life beyond his slavery. He overcame many obstacles, including being enslaved, yet he did not let those challenges stop him from seeking more knowledge and settling on Stoic philosophy.

Endurance and resilience are thematic aspects of Epictetus' Discourses, which the Stoic philosopher covered with an intense display of knowledge due to his life experience. He brought forth endurance and resilience as some of the ways that one can accept fate. He did not look at acceptance of fate as giving up on life but rather as accepting the inevitability of certain life circumstances and making the best out of time. Succumbing to the circumstances of life was not something Epictetus contemplated, and if there is something in his view that a person could succumb to, then it better be virtue and nothing else.

Epictetus cared about furthering the spirit of endurance and resilience and advocated steadfastness in adversity. In one way or another we are all bound to face adversity, what matters is how we come out of it. The only way for a Stoic like Epictetus to escape adversity was to be stronger and better. To a Stoic, adversity is an opportunity and not an obstacle, as it is often viewed because controlling the circumstances around you is not your responsibility.

Your responsibility lies in controlling your reaction to the circumstances around you.

Harmonious living with nature: The peace we often seek through the pursuit of external circumstances is often found within us. Epictetus has expressed that much, and it begins by living harmoniously with nature. As human beings, we are beneficiaries of nature and the providence of the universe. Therefore, our role and responsibility are not going against nature but rather harmonizing our existence with the needs of nature.

In Epictetus' teachings and submissions, the best way to live in harmony with nature's law is through embracing logic and reason in our actions. He contends that nature's law accommodates human needs up to the extent of sufficiency, and anything beyond that becomes destructive. For instance, the most common instant used by Epictetus and other Stoics is our constant desire for fame and external recognition when all that matters is within us. Nature's law is that excess is destructive; therefore, pursuing too much is destructive.

In the end, in Epictetus' Discourses, the most important lesson is that life can pose as many challenges as possible to you. It is nothing personal but rather how life is and how the universe or nature conducts its business. If you take it personally, you suffer; if you accept fate as it is and find ways to live in harmony with it, you will endure in the end, and something good will come out of it. Life can be as easy as your mind envisions it, or it can be as hard as you let your mind be prone to external influences that tend to spearhead the notion of life being hard.

Enchiridion

Enchiridion is mainly focused on those who want to become philosophers, and this is not to be taken to mean people who talk about various philosophies. In Epictetus's eyes, views, and teachings, a philosopher does more than talk about a particular philosophy; it is instead one who embodies that philosophy and practically leads the life embodied in the philosophy. Therefore, we do not remember men like Epictetus because they talked about Stoic philosophy but because they embodied it and gave it the practicality of life.

Like Discourses, Enchiridion is a documentation of Epictetus' Stoic teachings, and therefore, it takes shape through a thematic approach to Stoicism's most valued practices. The top one in the list is the dichotomy of control, and as explained in Discourses, we have control over the internal workings of our minds. Still, we do not have control over the external actions of other people. Epictetus implores us to keep our focus on what we can control as opposed to external influences. After all, we are the ones who truly know ourselves.

The most critical lesson in Epictetus' Enchiridion is to go with the flow. This means that you should never swim against the tide. Always go with the tide. This reflects the acceptance of things as they are and not as we want them. Often, things do not go the way you want. In Enchiridion, Epictetus implores you to accept things as they are.

That is the will of the universe and nature's law. Sometimes, it is easier to question what is happening in our lives. However, in the grand scheme of things, we are but mere specs. Certain things elude human perception and understanding. Therefore, accepting things as they are is a better way to be at peace with life than going against everything that seems to contradict our beliefs, wants, and desires.

Epictetus' Top Quotes

"Circumstances do not make a man; they reveal him."

In this powerful statement, Epictetus encapsulates a core principle of Stoic philosophy: our true character is not formed by our experiences but rather exposed through them. This quote teaches that while external conditions--be they adversity or prosperity--do not create our fundamental nature, they do play a crucial role in unveiling it.

Epictetus believed that hard times are particularly revealing. When faced with challenges, an individual's reactions can illuminate their virtues or shortcomings. For instance, adversity might bring out resilience and determination in one person, while provoking fear or anger in another. In each case, the circumstances do not forge these qualities but instead provide a context in which these traits manifest more clearly.

Furthermore, this perspective encourages self-awareness and personal accountability. By recognizing that our responses to life's situations reflect our true selves, we are prompted to cultivate strength and virtue proactively. Epictetus's insight urges us to focus less on blaming external factors and more on developing our inner resources, ensuring that our reactions enhance rather than diminish our integrity when times are tough.

This Stoic wisdom is about enduring life's trials and learning from them. Each challenge is an opportunity to discover more about ourselves and grow. In this way, Epictetus's teaching provides a roadmap for personal development, emphasizing that our greatest lessons often come not from what life throws at us but from how we respond.

"Man is not worried by real problems so much as his imagined anxieties about real problems."

Epictetus, a Stoic philosopher, highlighted that our greatest stresses often come not from the actual challenges we face but from the worries and fears we create about these challenges. We tend to expend much of our mental energy imagining what could go wrong rather than dealing with what is actually happening. This habit of forecasting problems can lead to unnecessary anxiety, causing us to suffer more in anticipation than we do in reality.

Epictetus taught that this tendency to dwell on potential negative outcomes is unhelpful and detrimental to our mental well-being. He advised that instead of fixating on what might happen in the future--a future over which we have little control--we should focus on the present. This means actively engaging with our current circumstances and reserving our emotional and mental resources for dealing with real, present issues as they arise.

By emphasizing the importance of staying in the moment, Epictetus encouraged his followers to let go of hypothetical worries and approach life's uncertainties calmly and practically. He believed that by doing so, we can significantly reduce our stress and enhance our ability to cope with whatever challenges we do encounter. Living in the present allows us to handle real problems more effectively when they occur, rather than becoming paralyzed by the fear of what could happen.

"The key to happiness is to learn to want what you already have."

Epictetus's wisdom in this quote guides us towards a profound understanding of happiness. He teaches that true contentment comes not from acquiring more, but from appreciating what we already possess. This principle is rooted in the Stoic belief that our desires can control us, leading to perpetual dissatisfaction and unrest if left unchecked.

By valuing what we have, we foster gratitude, which diminishes the insatiable yearning for more. Epictetus argues that this unchecked desire is a primary source of unhappiness; it disrupts our inner peace and catalyzes many of the vices that afflict society, such as greed, envy, and discontent.

Practicing contentment involves recognizing and celebrating our current blessings rather than fixating on what we lack or what others might possess. This mindset shift doesn't mean abandoning ambition or growth but pursuing them with a sense of wholeness rather than lack. By doing so, we can experience a more profound and stable form of happiness that is less dependent on external circumstances.

Epictetus's teaching encourages us to live with intention and mindfulness, focusing on the abundance present in our lives. Through contentment and gratitude, we can enhance our well-being and contribute to a more harmonious society. This approach aligns with the Stoic ideal of living according to nature, in harmony with the world and our true selves.

We can make the most of what we have by practicing contentment and gratitude.

Chapter 5

Epictetus' Emotional Equanimity

Men are disturbed not by things but by the views which they take of them. -Epictetus

Equanimity refers to the evenness of the mind. This concept is reinforced through Epictetus' words, works, and lectures. Stoicism often emphasizes the idea of apatheia, which brings out the importance of making logical decisions without letting the influence of emotions take over.

Epictetus Three Topoi

Epictetus outlined three fundamental principles that formed the basis of his Stoic philosophy and took center stage in his teachings. These three topics are further explained below.

The Discipline of Desire

In emphasizing the importance of mastering desire, Epictetus stressed that many human struggles stem from craving what is not possessed or shunning what is unwanted. Such yearnings and aversions only heighten anxiety, proving fruitless in resolving genuine issues.

His argument centers on aligning our desires and aversions with what we can control--our inner state. By harmonizing these with the controllable aspects of life, one can cultivate a serene, wise, and content existence.

Given historical accounts of Stoics overcoming adversity, one might question how Stoicism advocates accepting circumstances as they are. The crux lies in whether they combated hardships or stayed true to themselves until the trials passed. It's easy to mistake resilience and self-possession during tough times for direct opposition to those challenges.

During hardship, Stoics remained authentic, holding onto their core values and allowing virtues to steer them. Embracing fate, or 'amor fati,' a central tenet in Stoic philosophy, played a pivotal role.

Regarding 'amor fati,' accepting fate doesn't entail forfeiting oneself or succumbing when faced with adversity. Instead, it's a call to remain faithful to one's virtues, acknowledging internal influences and circumstances within one's control. The focus should not be on manipulating external events, as these lie beyond our sphere of influence. Therefore, accepting fate isn't about giving up; it's about standing firm in one's identity, embracing virtue, and staying true to oneself.

The Discipline of Action

In Stoic teachings specifically, Epictetus teaches that the concept of the discipline of action is anchored on our ability to control our actions. This is as opposed to external circumstances, which are, in one way or another, beyond our control.

The discipline of action impresses upon the Stoic concept of Eudaemonia or happiness. Ultimately, all that is required of us is to choose to wish each other happiness. It is nature's law that human beings work collaboratively in support of each other to achieve happiness as opposed to working against each other, which can only lead to division.

Our actions are the by-products of our choices. Epictetus then implores you to make your choices based on moral integrity and virtue. When a choice is virtuous and morally upright, there is a high chance that the resulting action will positively impact the lives of others or, at the very least, cause no harm.

The Discipline of Assent

This discipline is anchored on the exercising of careful judgment and discernment. The emphasis is on making decisions that are morally sound and virtuous. Since our thoughts and beliefs highly influence our choices, it is preferable that we first exercise that discernment in our thoughts and beliefs before we extend it to our actions. If our thoughts and beliefs are well discerned and judged, our actions will be well thought out and virtuous.

How do you attain careful judgment and discernment? You can arrive at that by embracing the Stoic principle of wisdom. Engage every faculty of your mind through logic and careful reasoning. This helps you maintain vigilance and watch over your thoughts and beliefs.

Remember What Is Within Your Control

According to Stoic philosophy, and as argued and taught by almost all the great Stoic philosophers, everything is anchored on the dichotomy of control. It is glued to the idea that there is much to do about what is within our control and very little to do about what is not.

Epictetus on Control

Like all other great Stoic philosophers, Epictetus had his own ideas and contentions about control--some unique to himself and some anchored on the general principles of Stoicism taught by other philosophers.

Epictetus learned control through experience. When he was born and raised in slavery, his masters controlled everything around him. They controlled what he ate and how he spent his time. They even controlled who he interacted with, what he read, and how he read it. The one thing that they could not control was his mind. As far as his mind and thoughts were concerned, that was his territory, and he could not let anyone get in there.

By being in control of our minds and not letting others control our thoughts or influence our actions, we can understand the Stoic dichotomy of control and Epictetus' approach to the concept of control. He did not focus on what lay beyond him; instead, he focused his energies on what was within him.

How to Put the Dichotomy of Control Into Practice

The significance of the dichotomy of control has been emphasized repeatedly. However, often, we have not been told how to put this great principle of gaining control of our circumstances into use. The following are some of the ways you can set the dichotomy of control into use:

• Identify what in your life you can gain control over, or you already have control over. The dichotomy of control is anchored on gaining control over things within you; these include your thoughts, emotions, and reactions to other people's sentiments about you and their actions towards you.

• Acceptance of what you cannot control: Acknowledging that there are many things that you cannot control goes a long way toward ensuring that you are aware of what lies within your reach. Acceptance is critical in taking a step toward mastering those things or internal factors that you can control.

• Avoid attachment to outcomes: As a human being, it is only natural that, at times, you would desire a certain outcome in certain situations. However, having already acknowledged that outcomes are often beyond your control, you must avoid anchoring your expectations on outcomes you have no control over. Regarding outcomes, embracing whatever outcome you get is essential to avoid attachment. If you unknowingly find yourself attached to a particular outcome, then letting go of that attachment is appropriate.

Below is a step-by-step illustration of how you can use the dichotomy of control momentarily and with practicality.

You may start with a small writing exercise by selecting a situation or event that recently gave you a hard time. However, it is advisable to choose an event that is not too overwhelming. Even Epictetus often emphasizes starting with things you can easily handle before transitioning to complex ones.

The next step is to open a blank page in a book, notebook, writing pad, or anywhere else you may feel comfortable writing. Draw two columns, labeling the first column 'things within my control' and the second column ' things beyond my control.'

The next step is briefly describing why you chose the event and then listing its components. As you list those components, ensure you put them in the relevant column, either the ' things within my control' or ' the things beyond my control' column.

This list you have formed gives you an objectively clear list of the things you can focus on. In this case, you should focus on those you listed as being within your control.

Apatheia

Apatheia refers to the state of being free from negative emotions. Often, apatheia is mistaken for the need to get rid of emotions, especially by those who practice Stoicism. However, apatheia does not mean a lack of emotions or the suppression of emotions. To a Stoic, apatheia is a state of balance between rationality and emotion. Emotions will exist and be alive and well, but they will not be factored into any decision-making.

Epictetus on Apatheia

The concept of apatheia is widely acclaimed in the Stoic world, and Epictetus had good insights into it. Epictetus considered pain or painful moments much less painful if no emotions or opinions were added to them.

He often believed and taught that a good life is attainable if you develop less inclination to passion and emotions. He, therefore, argued that apatheia does not mean the absence of passion or emotion but rather the non-adherence and non-conformity to them.

Epictetus' belief in the concept of apatheia was so deep that it is said that at one point when his master was punishing him, he twisted his leg. Epictetus warned his master that his leg would eventually break if he continued to twist it. When it did eventually, he looked at his master and said, " I told you it will break," without a show of emotion or pain. It has been said that it is how Epictetus became crippled, even though others have made arguments that it was out of illness.

Epictetus believed that emotions, opinions, and passions made pain worse or took the balance out of life. Therefore, he advocated for a life where those things were not at the center stage without invalidating their importance. After all, he understood that they play a part. He emphasized that one had to cultivate a mindset of tranquility and rationality.

How to Practice Apatheia

The following is a step-by-step guide on how you can practice apatheia.

• Take charge of your emotions.

Whenever you are facing adversity, do not let your emotions control you or the situation. Instead, embrace rationality and take sound and logical steps.

• Embrace objectivity.

Do not let events throw you off balance so that you are unable to analyze them and devise a plan for moving forward.

After all, "Don't let the force of an impression when it first hits you knock you off your feet; just say to it: Hold on a moment. Let me see who you are and what you represent. Let me put you to the test."

To reiterate Epictetus's words above, do not let first impressions of situations, events, conditions, or people fool you. Take your time and put them through a logical test.

• Develop a contemptuous approach.

This means treating any obstacles that come your way contemptuously. This will enable you to overcome them because you will have eliminated the emotion of fear through contempt.

Let's say you want to quit drinking wine. You first refer to it contemptuously to remove the fuzz around it and make it lose its importance. For instance, you can say, 'Wine is just overstayed grapes.'

• Live in the moment.

When you embrace every moment as it comes, it makes it easier to take a rational approach to events of the moment. Do not waste the present moment anticipating the following or coming moment.

• Focus on the opportunities.

Whatever challenges may come your way at any moment, always find the opportunity within. This will help you not fixate on the challenge itself but rather the opportunity it presents, helping you maintain rationality even in the most emotionally tempting moments.

Helpful Hacks for Emotional Control

The following are some of the things you can do to keep your emotions in control easily:

Breathwork

Breathwork refers to the practice of consciously controlling and focusing on your breathing patterns. This deliberate focus on the breath serves as a powerful tool to influence one's physical, mental, and emotional states. By becoming aware of how we breathe and learning to regulate it, we can trigger significant changes in our body and mind.

The practice of breathwork encompasses a variety of techniques, each designed to achieve specific outcomes. These can range from calming the nervous system and reducing stress to energizing the body and enhancing mental clarity. Techniques often involve patterns such as deep breathing, controlled inhalations and exhalations, and holding the breath for different durations.

Breathwork is a standalone practice and an integral component of various therapeutic and fitness disciplines, including yoga, meditation, and some psychotherapeutic techniques. It is used to help individuals manage anxiety, improve concentration, and boost overall well-being.

Taking deep breaths, a common breathwork practice, is particularly effective in activating the body's natural relaxation response. This can help alleviate stress, reduce blood pressure, and promote a sense of calm. Regular practice of breathwork can lead to improved emotional resilience and a healthier state of mind.

In summary, breathwork offers a readily accessible way to enhance physical health, control emotional responses, and achieve a clearer state of mind. It empowers individuals to positively impact their physiological and psychological states, fostering overall health and well-being

• Sensory grounding.

Sensory grounding requires you to wire and focus all your attention on your senses--all six senses. You use sensory stimuli like smell, taste, and hearing to cultivate mindfulness. This helps reduce stress and regulate your emotions.

One sensory grounding exercise is the 5-4-3-2-1 technique; in this technique, the goal is to name five things you can see: four things you can touch, three things you can hear, two things you can smell, and one thing you can taste. By the time you are done with this exercise, you will afford yourself a worthwhile distraction from whatever is stressing you.

Acceptance of Your Emotions

Understanding and mastering your emotions is a critical step towards accepting them as they are. Acceptance means acknowledging your feelings without judgment, regardless of whether they are comfortable or difficult. Accepting your emotions prevents them from overpowering you, and you can manage them more effectively.

When you embrace your emotions, you recognize that they are a normal part of the human experience, not something to be suppressed or feared. This acceptance allows you to respond to your feelings with clarity and wisdom, rather than reacting impulsively. For instance, recognizing and accepting feelings of anger or sadness can help you understand their origins and address the underlying issues constructively.

Developing Resilience in the Face of Adversity

Emotional acceptance is closely linked to resilience--the ability to bounce back from challenges and adapt to stress and adversity. Accepting your emotions builds a stronger foundation for facing difficult situations. This is because you are not wasting energy fighting your feelings but instead using that energy to confront the actual challenges at hand.

Resilient individuals are able to experience a range of emotions and still take positive actions. They do not let their emotions control their decisions; instead, they acknowledge their feelings and use them as signals to guide their actions. This ability to manage and learn from emotions is essential in developing resilience and maintaining mental health.

In summary, the acceptance of your emotions forms the cornerstone of emotional intelligence and resilience. It equips you with the tools to navigate the complexities of life, enabling you to respond to adversity with strength and flexibility. This process enhances your ability to cope with current challenges and prepares you for future obstacles.

Epictetus on Mindset

A mindset is a set of values, virtues, perceptions, and trains of thought that shape your thinking, interpretation of events, and general approach to life. If anything, Epictetus impresses upon the power of the mind through his teachings. Ultimately, it is the one true thing we have that no one else has control over unless we let them have that control.

Essentially, Epictetus advocated for a mindful and robust mindset--one that is focused on the present with no prefixed judgments. To attain this mindset, one must be fully aware of one's thoughts, emotions, and sensations in the present moment.

A result of this robust mindset that Epictetus and Stoicism generally advocated for is inner peace. You accept yourself as you are and keep off worrying about what impression others may have of you.

How to Respond to Failure or Misfortune

Life will always bring along eventualities like failure and diverse brands of misfortune. However, that is not a call for you to give in to those misfortunes and folds; it is a call to positive action and logical reactions. After all, " An ignorant person is inclined to blame others for his misfortune. To blame oneself is proof of progress. But the wise man never has to blame another or himself."

Stoicism implores us to acknowledge that life happens and that we must remain ourselves even when misfortune strikes. In Stoic teachings, a person conquers adversity not by being clever and running away from it but rather by accepting it. This is emphasized in the Stoic principle of ' Amor fati,' which loosely translates to' accepting fate. ' Accepting fate means that you remain yourself regardless of the circumstances.

Exercises

Growth Mindset Journal Prompts

Developing a growth mindset involves embracing challenges, learning from feedback, and persisting in the face of setbacks. Use the following journal prompts to cultivate this mindset and enhance your personal growth:

Learning from the Past: Reflect on an unpleasant past experience. How can you view this event as a learning opportunity rather than a setback? What lessons can be drawn from this experience to foster your growth?

Overcoming Internal Criticism: Consider the internal critic who influences your thoughts. How is this critic holding you back from achieving your goals? What steps can you take to challenge this internal voice and move forward?

Attitude Towards Growth: Describe your current attitude towards personal growth. Is it optimistic, skeptical, or indifferent? How does this attitude influence your daily behavior and long-term development?

Comfort Zones and Growth: Identify an area in your life where you feel stuck. Why do you think you have remained in this space? What might be the benefits of stepping out of this comfort zone, and what first step could you take?

Resistance to Change: Consider any changes you are currently resisting in your life. Why might you be resisting these changes? What are the potential positive outcomes if you embrace these changes instead?

Self-Care Practices: Reflect on your current self-care practices. What activities do you engage in that help maintain your mental, physical, and emotional health? How do these practices support your personal growth and resilience?

What kind of attitude do you have towards self-development, and how does that attitude affect your growth?

These prompts have been carefully curated to guide you toward a growth mindset. A growth mindset encourages you to always look at the positive and the possible rather than the negative and the impossible.

The next chapter covers the story of Marcus Aurelius, or as he is commonly referred to as, the philosopher king. He is one of Rome's last true rulers who stood for virtue and righteousness. He was an ardent Stoic and an inspirational figure during his time, throughout history, and in modern times.

Hey there, fellow reader!

You've just sailed past the halfway mark of "THE TRIAD OF STOICISM," diving deep into the timeless wisdom of Marcus Aurelius, Seneca, and Epictetus. Impressive, right? Now, how about taking a tiny detour to do something extraordinary?

Let's chat about the superpower of leaving a review!

Ever wonder how a few simple words can light up someone's day or guide them to make a great decision? Well, your thoughts on this book could be that guiding star for countless others on the brink of a Stoic adventure!

Quick question for you: Have you ever picked up a book because a review made you think, "Hey, this sounds like just what I need!"? Imagine being that beacon for someone else!

Leaving a review is your chance to pass on the golden nuggets of wisdom you've gleaned from the stoic masters. It's not just about giving feedback; it's about sharing an experience that could help others lead a more serene and purposeful life. It's about connecting your journey to theirs, stitching a tapestry of shared human experience through words.

Here's the scoop: Your insights are invaluable! Whether it's a powerful quote that struck a chord, a chapter that turned your day around, or just the overall impact the book has had on you—your shared experience can light the way for others. Plus, it helps us understand what hits home with our readers so we can keep the good stuff coming!

To leave your feedback:

1. Open your camera app.
2. Point your mobile device at the QR code below.
3. The review page will appear in your web browser.

Or visit: https://www.amazon.com/dp/B0DQKKNHTT

Thank you!

So, here's my ask: Would you take a moment to leave an honest review of "THE TRIAD OF STOICISM"? Just a few sentences describing what you think of the book and how it has influenced you. It's easy! Simply pop over or wherever you grabbed your copy, and let your thoughts be known. Your review could be the reason someone decides to dip their toes into the tranquil waters of Stoicism.

The impact? Massive! Every review helps spread Stoic philosophy's wisdom further, touching lives and making a real difference. It's like handing over a tool that can build resilience and peace in someone's life.

The best part? By sharing your insights, you're not just helping others; you're also enriching your own life. It's the Stoic way—creating value for others, enriching the world one thoughtful action at a time. Plus, who knows? Your kind words could come back to you the next time you're on the hunt for a good read in the form of recommendations tailored just for you by fellow thoughtful readers.

Ready to make a difference? It's review time! Let's help others find a little wisdom and serenity. Who knows whose life you might change with just a few keystrokes? Thank you for being a part of this journey and for helping to spread the spirit of Stoicism far and wide. Let's keep the circle of learning and inspiration flowing!

Chapter 6

Meditations of the Philosopher King Marcus Aurelius

The impediment to action advances action. What stands in the way becomes the way. -Marcus Aurelius

Marcus Aurelius' Reign of Virtue

Born in 161 AD, Marcus Aurelius is perhaps Rome's one true benevolent leader. This can be seen through his actions, affection, and the true care he extended to the Roman people. He led them with grace, virtue, and dignity.

Marcus Aurelius was born into a Roman Patrician family, and his adoptive father, Titus Aurelius Antoninus, did not spare any expense to ensure that Marcus' passion for education was fully satisfied. He hired the best teachers to facilitate Marcus' educational journey and prepare him for the leadership of the great Roman empire.

Marcus, in return, did not disappoint. He took education seriously and passionately. He took a greater interest in Stoic philosophy and is recognized as one of Stoicism's most revered proponents. His life was a life of virtue and a revered appreciation for philosophy.

He did not just learn philosophy; Marcus embodied it. In the end, he was widely recognized as the philosopher King, leaving behind great, widely, and wildly celebrated works like 'The Meditations', a book widely acclaimed by great men and ordinary men in equal measure.

During Marcus' reign as emperor of Rome, he was characterized as a leader of impeccable character and had a flawless approach to society's needs. He cared for his people and delivered for them genuinely, effectively, and to the best of his ability. He was a reign of peace, prosperity, fairness, and tranquility.

The kind that was never to be seen in Rome again after his reign and his demise ended. He was revered, and his legacy stands to this day. Great world leaders have often found him to be the perfect inspiration for them, and it has paid off.

Marcus Aurelius and His Perspective on Stoicism

Amongst Stoicism's greatest proponents, Marcus Aurelius stands as a pillar and an inspiration. He learned the philosophy, embodied it, and incorporated it into his actions. On his perspective on Stoicism, Marcus Aurelius emphasized the following principles of Stoic philosophy:

- **Acceptance and providence.**

Marcus Aurelius was an ardent believer of nature's way and a providential universe. We are mere specs in the grand scheme of things, and as such, we need to live in harmony with nature's way and what nature will provide. In all that, he emphasized that every individual should be able to accept their fate at the end of the day because there is no other way.

- **He viewed virtue as the highest possible good.**

If every individual in a society embraces virtue and lives a righteous life, then the result will be a virtuous and upright society. Marcus Aurelius emphasized this. To him and other Stoic Philosophers, virtue was the highest good.

He believed in living a life of virtue characterized by wisdom, courage, and justice. These were the things that he believed could lead him to prosperity, and by embodying these principles, Marcus Aurelius experienced prosperity exponentially. At the end of the day, he was an Emperor of the great Roman Empire. He was good, and he did well.

• He advocated for endurance and resilience.

Marcus Aurelius practiced the Stoic virtues of endurance and resilience and frequently advocated and emphasized them to others. He believed that adversity is not the end of life as we know it but rather a part of life.

Although your circumstances may change, you do not need to change yourself or your virtuous approach to life. Marcus emphasized remaining steadfast and unshaken amid difficulties and unpredictable times. For him, obstacles were not blockers and derailers of achievement or destiny; they were the way to achievement and destiny.

• He emphasized impermanence and detachment.

Life is transient; we are only mere travelers on this long train. We alight at different points, and the train continues with no stopping. Marcus Aurelius recognized this transient nature of life and often emphasized the essence of detaching from our material possessions and things beyond our control.

He advocated focusing on our inner selves because you never know when the train will stop, and it is your turn to alight. From that perspective of the unpredictability of life and the inevitability of death, Marcus encouraged people to embrace detachment from things and focus on embracing life as it is in the present.

In the end, it is only wise to acknowledge that material things can vanish. If we are too attached to them, we will experience unnecessary suffering, which will make our lives unfulfilling.

• He strongly advocated for mindfulness and self-reflection.

In Stoicism, self-reflection is the perfect way to converse with yourself and soul search. You lay bare your inner self for your mind to assess. It helps you restructure, re-energize, and rewire your life for the better. Mindfulness helps create a conducive environment for your subconscious and conscious minds to have an open and enlightening conversation.

You have clarity and inner peace by the time you get out of a mindfulness and self-reflection session. Marcus Aurelius advocated for this--he believed in it and practiced it as often as possible. It contributed much to his well-being and promoted a virtuous way of life for him.

The Works of Marcus Aurelius

Meditations

Meditation is a collection of Marcus Aurelius' writings recorded in his journal. The works revolve around his daily routine, how he incorporated Stoicism into his daily life activities, and his leadership role as Emperor of Rome. He wrote the Meditations during his reign as Emperor and never intended the work to be published since it was a personal record of his insights and philosophical words.

In the end, the work was found among his preserved items after his passing on. It was then released to the public and has since been widely acclaimed. The works have inspired persons of all walks, professions, and cultural orientations. Marcus Aurelius' Meditations is Stoicism' most celebrated work. The book is divided into twelve books, each representing each journal that Marcus Aurelius filled. They have analyzed and summarized as follows:

Chapter by Chapter Summary of Marcus Aurelius' Meditations: Book 1

This is Marcus' first book of the twelve and represents his first journal. He started it during his virtuous journey and Stoic adherence. His reflections are anchored on the importance of being true to oneself and living by virtue.

Outside opinions and circumstances did not carry much weight and did not influence important aspects of his life. In this first journal, Marcus Aurelius emphasizes the importance of inner strength. This inner strength saw him maintain his principles and strict adherence to them.

Meditations: Book 2

In Book 2, the second chapter and journal from Marcus Aurelius' Meditations, he wrote about life's fleeting nature and death's inevitability. In this book, Marcus impresses upon living in the present moment. He not only advocates for living in the present but also does so virtuously with integrity and purpose.

Marcus believed that life was in the present, not the past or future. It is the present that you have control over; the past belongs to the past, and the future to God. This means that the present is where life is. The circumstances of your life are right with you; you do not have to seek them from the future or the past. Worrying about tomorrow or the past will have you worrying before you even encounter the major challenge.

Meditations: Book 3

In his third journal, Marcus Aurelius dwells on detachment from external circumstances. Marcus had come to understand the impermanence of the external circumstances of life and material things. These are all things whose existence you cannot truly be certain of controlling. Today, you could have riches and wealth and lose them all the next day. Other external circumstances include people's opinions and perceptions of you.

Today, they might say nice things about you, but tomorrow, they might turn you into their enemy. If you are attached to their good words about you and the next day, you hear them say all negative words, you will go through a lot of mental turmoil. Therefore, throughout this book, Marcus impresses upon the importance of mental resilience.

Under this pretext, Marcus insists that it pays off to detach from external things and focus on personal responsibility and internal tranquility because those are factors within your reach and control. After all, "If thou pained by an external thing, it is not this thing that disturbs thee, but thy judgment about it. And it is in thy power to wipe out this judgment now. But if anything in thy disposition gives thy pain, who hinders thee from correcting thy opinion?"

Meditations: Book 4

In book 4, Marcus Aurelius delves into the concept of self-discipline and the importance of overcoming negative emotions such as anger and fear. These feelings are of no true importance apart from holding your mind hostage and depriving you of your inner tranquility.

Marcus emphasizes the significance of building order from within. The timeless Stoic practice of self-discipline achieves this. In this book, Marcus reminds himself to curb his appetites for fame, fortune, and praise. He emphasizes it to everyone else as it aligns you with the universe's needs and harmonizes your existence with them.

He delves into the concept of rationality and its significance in approaching the nuances and intricacies of life rather than using emotions like anger. In his view, emotions are irrational and often have adverse outcomes, which can put you into mental turmoil instead of taking it away.

Meditations: Book 5

In Book 5 of his "Meditations," Marcus Aurelius delves into the virtue of humility, emphasizing its critical role amidst the impermanence and unpredictability of life. This section of his philosophical diary reflects on the importance of humility in recognizing and accepting one's limitations.

Marcus discusses how humility allows us to see ourselves as part of a larger whole, rather than as isolated entities. This perspective is vital in managing our desires and expectations, as it aligns our personal ambitions with the reality of our circumstances and the nature of the universe. He advises that this recognition of our own limitations should not be seen as a source of discouragement but as a guide to living within the bounds of what is realistically achievable and morally right.

Moreover, Marcus connects humility with the Stoic acceptance of fate. He believes that understanding and accepting the limits imposed by nature helps us to cope with life's changes and challenges more gracefully. This acceptance is not passive resignation but an active engagement with life, taking action where we can and relinquishing control where it is beyond our reach.

According to Marcus, humility also fosters resilience. By acknowledging that we do not have control over everything, we can focus our efforts on our responses and attitudes toward the events of life that are within our control. This shift in focus helps to reduce anxiety about the future and regret over the past, anchoring us more firmly in the present moment.

Book 5 of "Meditations" offers profound insights into how humility intersects with Stoic principles. Marcus Aurelius presents humility not as a weakness but as a strength that helps us navigate the inherent uncertainties of life with dignity and composure.

Just as life is temporary, so are the pleasures that come with it. In connection with this notion, Marcus looks at the interconnection between work and leisure.

He emphasizes the importance of allocating time for both work and leisure.

Meditations: Book 6

In Book 6 of "Meditations," Marcus Aurelius delves into contemplating the cosmos and our place within it, emphasizing the transient nature of existence and the guidance of universal providence. This book serves as a profound reminder that life is both given and taken by the universe and that forces beyond our individual control ultimately dictate our time.

Marcus reflects on the concept that all lives, including his own, begin and conclude within the parameters set by the cosmos. This understanding leads him to a stoic acceptance that nothing outside of performing his duty should hold importance. His commitment to duty, defined by his role as emperor and a rational being, underscores a central Stoic belief in focusing on actions over which one has control and detaching from those one does not.

Moreover, Marcus reiterates his reliance on philosophy as a vital tool for resilience. He views philosophical practice as a field of study and a practical framework for living virtuously and managing life's adversities. Philosophy offers him a refuge and a method to reconnect with his duties and responsibilities, ensuring that his actions are aligned with reason and virtue.

Meditations: Book 7

In Book 7 of "Meditations," Marcus Aurelius explores the transient nature of life and the inevitability of death, urging a perspective that emphasizes the importance of harmony and unity. He contemplates the fleeting aspects of human existence and the eventual return of all things to the logos--the underlying reason and order of the universe.

Marcus reflects on human behaviors and the commonalities that bind people together. He emphasizes that despite superficial differences, the fundamental experiences of life and death unite all humans. He argues that This shared condition should inspire us to live in cooperation and peace rather than conflict. By recognizing our shared destiny, we can cultivate a sense of empathy and solidarity with others.

The notion of living in accordance with cosmic providence is central to this book. Marcus suggests that since life is temporary and its duration uncertain, our focus should be on living virtuously and in service to others. This alignment with the cosmos is not merely a duty but a source of deep fulfillment and stability in the face of life's uncertainties.

Marcus also explores the concept that, in the end, everything will be reabsorbed into the logos, reminding us that our actions and conflicts are fleeting and ultimately subordinate to the greater order of the universe. This perspective encourages a detachment from petty grievances and a deeper commitment to actions that are aligned with the greater good.

Meditations: Book 8

In Book 8 of "Meditations," Marcus Aurelius shares his vision of what constitutes a good life, emphasizing virtue over material wealth or luxury. He explores the foundational principles of Stoic ethics, which hinge on a clear understanding of good and evil, and how these concepts guide the Stoic path to a virtuous life.

Marcus posits that a good life is achieved not through accumulating external possessions or status but through cultivating inner virtues such as wisdom, justice, courage, and moderation. He stresses the importance of discerning what is truly good--actions and characteristics that contribute positively to oneself and to society--and what is evil--those that harm or detract from the common welfare.

According to Marcus, understanding good and evil is crucial because it directs one's actions and decisions towards virtue. He argues that once an individual grasps the true nature of good and evil, they are equipped to apply this knowledge in their daily lives. This application involves making choices that are in harmony with one's own nature as a rational being and with the nature of the universe, which Marcus believes is governed by a rational and providential order.

Furthermore, Marcus encourages constant self-reflection and vigilance in maintaining virtuous conduct. He reminds himself and his readers that living a good life requires ongoing effort and the readiness to face each situation with moral clarity and ethical resolve. This includes being just in one's dealings, showing courage in the face of adversity, exercising restraint in pleasures, and maintaining a demeanor of calm rationality regardless of external circumstances.

Meditations: Book 9

In Book 9 of Meditations, Marcus Aurelius delves into the ethical challenges and potential pitfalls that can disrupt a virtuous life. He identifies five key sins that can lead individuals astray: injustice, lying, the excessive pursuit of pleasure, the avoidance of pain, and the fear of pain. Each of these, he argues, stems from improper handling of one's impulses and a failure to act according to reason.

Marcus emphasizes that certain experiences--pain, pleasure, fame, and death--are inherently morally neutral. They do not possess moral qualities in themselves but gain ethical significance through our responses to them. This Stoic idea highlights that it is not the external events or circumstances that define our moral character, but how we choose to react to them.

Injustice: Committing injustice goes against the Stoic principle of living in harmony with others. Marcus believes that justice is a natural virtue, and acting against it disrupts both personal integrity and social harmony.

Lying: Deception is seen as a departure from the Stoic commitment to truth and authenticity. For Marcus, honesty fortifies the soul and aligns it with the rational order of the universe.

Pursuing Pleasure: Overindulgence in pleasure can enslave us to our desires, leading to a loss of rational control and a deviation from virtuous living.

Avoiding Pain: Similarly, going to great lengths to avoid pain can make us cowardly and prevent us from facing necessary aspects of life bravely and with integrity.

Fearing Pain: Excessive fear of pain can cripple our ability to act according to reason and can lead us to make decisions that compromise our moral values.

By addressing these five sins, Marcus encourages a stoic discipline over one's emotions and actions, urging a life that consistently reflects virtue regardless of external circumstances. This approach calls for a deep understanding of the nature of things as neutral and the cultivation of personal virtues to navigate life's challenges.

Meditations: Book 10

In book 10, Marcus reminds himself that he is part of a whole. This reminds him to work for the benefit of the whole society and not just himself. He emphasizes that human beings are like parts of a body, and each part plays a role in achieving the purpose that the whole body seeks to achieve.

Whenever one part works against the others, that becomes an obstacle to achieving that purpose. Therefore, we are supposed to work together to achieve the universe's purpose. Any actions not for the common good are in contravention of that purpose.

Meditations: Book 11

In Book 11 of Meditations, Marcus Aurelius deepens his examination of the rational soul, emphasizing its pivotal role in shaping a life aligned with Stoic principles.

He enunciates a vision where the rational soul, which he considers the essence of human identity, is self-governing and acutely aware of its interconnectedness with the universe.

Marcus posits that the rational soul should guide one's life, making decisions based on reason and virtue rather than impulse or emotion. This guidance is crucial because it aligns individual actions with the universal reason, or Logos, which Marcus believes orchestrates the cosmos. By adhering to this rational principle, individuals fulfill their nature as rational beings and contribute positively to the order of the world.

Marcus also reflects on the challenges that confront the rational soul, such as distractions, adversities, and internal conflicts. He provides guidance on maintaining composure and integrity in the face of such challenges, advocating for a life that consistently reflects rational judgment and ethical consistency. According to Marcus, the rational soul thrives on clarity of thought and purpose, which in turn fosters a life of peace and fulfillment.

Meditations: Book 12

In book 12, Marcus contemplates death as an inevitable eventuality everyone should be ready for. Therefore, he prays that when his time to die comes, may it do so calmly. He emphasizes the reason we should accept and prepare for death.

Quotes from Marcus Aurelius

"Our life is what our thoughts make it."

"Adapt yourself to the life you have been given, and truly love the people with whom destiny has surrounded you."

This profound statement encapsulates the Stoic principles of acceptance and cosmic providence. According to Stoic philosophy, much of our life is shaped by forces beyond our control, and recognizing this can lead to a more harmonious existence. By accepting the life we have been given, we align ourselves with the cosmos, acknowledging that our individual circumstances are part of a larger, predetermined plan.

The concept of cosmic providence suggests that everything in the universe, including our own lives and the people in them, follows a rational order and purpose. From this perspective, acceptance is not passive resignation but an active embrace of our roles and relationships. This acceptance is crucial as it enables us to fulfill our duties with diligence and compassion, guided by the understanding that our paths are woven into the fabric of a greater design.

Loving the people destiny places in our lives is a reflection of this acceptance. It emphasizes the Stoic ideal that virtues like love and kindness are not dependent on the qualities of others but are expressions of our own character. By loving and supporting those around us, we contribute to the common good and embody the virtues that Stoicism holds dear.

Moreover, this quote encourages a perspective shift from resistance to cooperation with the natural flow of life. We find deeper meaning and satisfaction by adapting to our circumstances and caring genuinely for others. Through these relationships and roles, we can best express our virtues and work towards the purposes the universe has intended for us.

Chapter 7

Marcus Aurelius' Majestic Mindful Mastery

If you are distressed by anything external, the pain is not due to the thing itself but to your estimate of it, and you have the power to revoke this at any moment. -Marcus Aurelius

Love Your Fate

Fate is the one thing in life we can never escape. Despite whatever dispositions we may have, our fates are predetermined. They are already written among the stars. Whether we embrace those fates or not, our choices are limited; we only have a single choice. We will face our fates in one way or another.

How we approach our fates ultimately determines how much we suffer. It doesn't matter whether you accept your fate; it will not change. Marcus Aurelius lived his life fully accepting fate; he lived one day at a time, knowing he could never change his fate. His only option was to embrace it and curate himself, his habits, and his life to best handle his fate.

We draw sufficient inspiration from Marcus Aurelius's handling of fate; embracing fate is our best bet. How, then, do we embrace fate, and what fate are we being told to embrace and accept?

Fate is a development of events beyond our control. This is even though these events beyond our control are directly impactful, sometimes damaging, and sometimes developmental in our lives. What makes fate so damning and essentially a bit scary to us mere mortals is that we have no control over it. That predisposition is a preserve of the Almighty God, the gods, and the universe; the point here is that a supernatural being is pulling all the strings.

We are merely controlled players engaging in a game of tassel with life. There are no winners or losers; people are inevitably waiting for fate to take its course.

Having that in mind now brings you back to seeking answers for what it is that you need to do to live in full embrace of your fate. Enjoy each moment of your life like it was the last, with minimal regard for things you cannot control. The answer lies in loving fate, claiming it, and prospering in it. If prosperity is not in your fate, you will still not be prone to suffering because you would have already embraced it. That is what Marcus Aurelius did when he was appointed Emperor of Rome, the world's most powerful empire.

A station that was too high and had a lot of responsibility. He had to accept that that was the path the universe had chosen for him, and he had to live in harmony with that path. This is all visible in his 'Meditations'. Marcus woke up every day ready to do what he was born to do. He believed that everything he was to do, he was born to do. He implores you to handle your fate the same way. It is how it is, and you will take it as such. The more you embrace it, the easier it becomes each day.

Aurelius on Amor Fati

Amor Fati, a phrase that generally translates to 'the love fate', was practiced, popularized, and taught by great Stoics, among them Marcus Aurelius. Even though neither Marcus nor Epictetus or any other one of the great Stoics coined this phrase, they lived in the spirit of this phrase. This phrase was originally by German philosopher Fredrick Nietzsche, who often admitted he wanted only to be a yes-sayer. Do not question anything or life's events, but rather make something positive out of them and respond with utmost gratitude.

Back to Marcus Aurelius and his stand on 'Amor Fati.' In his journal every morning, Marcis would write words of encouragement grounded on the Stoic spirit. These words were to remind him of his role in the universe. These are the words that later became the excellent book' Meditations' by none other than the great emperor and Stoic himself. His stance on 'Amor Fati' was no different from those of other Stoics; however, from his Meditations, we can get an in-depth understanding of what the love fate meant to him and how it influenced his life and the love of life thereof.

Another way of looking at 'Amor Fati' is as the ability to embrace the same things repeatedly. As a human being, chances are you are drawn to the same challenges and excitements, and no matter how much you try to escape, it is inescapable. Fate is what it is, and what is sometimes can not be changed.

If anything, Marcus Aurelius taught us the lesson of 'amor fati' so well throughout his life. Each day, he woke up with the same passion and did the same thing: led the people of Rome diligently, knowing deep down that he had to love that role because it was his fate.

You are implored to love your fate as well. What situation do you find yourself in? Is it possible to change it? It is not fate if it can be changed. Fate is the absolute and final chain of events that the universe or God chooses for you.

Ultimately, you come to live in harmony with the fact that you are not more special than the rest of the world. The only difference is that your fate is unique to you. Collectively, our fates are in alignment with the cosmic needs and purpose of the universe. When it is your turn to play your part in that purpose, love of fate should be your absolute and inevitable motivation.

Essentially, the 'Amor Fati' concept is Stoicism's unique way of telling you that life will happen without your permission. It is a call to positive action and eliminating regret and despair. Turns and twists will be there, and you will live through them however you will. The best way is to live them; however, they come with a certain determination in yourself to give it the best you have got.

Mastering the Art of Acceptance

Fate presents itself, and then you learn to love it as it is. After you learn to love it, you immerse yourself in accepting it. Acceptance is the other key element of the general concept of 'Amor Fati.' The sooner you accept the series of random events that the universe aligns you with, the easier it is to live a fulfilling life.

Sometimes, the universe has a way of reminding humanity of who is truly in charge. We often go ahead and affix ourselves with wild plans, which probably just end up being wild notions--figments of our fertile imaginations. Nothing is wrong with that; we are merely human beings, and the greatest power we have, at least to feel in control of our lives, is the power of a fertile imagination.

However, after our fertile imagination has done its work, the universe can undo it. It can either be a subtle humbling or a hugely humbling experience to remind us of who is the boss, and that, more often than not, circles back to the universe being the boss.

Affirmations

The following are some of the affirmations that you can embrace to aid you in effecting your acceptance of fate and the love of it:

The present moment is all I have; I will fully embrace its twists and turns.

All experiences, whether positive or negative, are an opportunity to learn.

I am not afraid of challenges; I welcome them and will turn them into stepping stones on my journey toward achieving wisdom and resilience.

I trust in myself to navigate whatever challenges life presents.

I have now surrendered to the flow of life.

I will be in harmony with the things I cannot control.

Everything happens for a reason; I will not question my fate.

Your Opinion Shapes Reality

Our opinions about life and other essential things pertinent to life shape our realities. When our opinions start influencing our life choices, our realities fundamentally rely on our opinions.

Our choices become responsible for the various outcomes of our lives. It is also true that our choices directly result from our reactions to other people's actions. Opinions are generally word-for-word scripted perceptions of how we view various aspects of life. These perceptions, or rather opinions, are the ones that, in the end, become the realities that form the very fabric of the intricacies of our lives.

How to Take Responsibility for Your Happiness

Happiness is a foundational concept of Stoic philosophy. It is the bedrock of pursuing a virtuous life, as emphasized in Stoicism. As often emphasized in Stoic philosophy, living a righteous life is synonymous with a happy life.

Why would great philosophers such as Marcus Aurelius and Seneca equate happiness to virtue? Were they wrong, or are we the ones who are wrong in equating pleasure to happiness?

The objective truth is that happiness blooms from within when one lives a virtuous life. The happiness that comes from pursuing pleasure and wild adventure is merely a wild goose chase based on external gratification. Therefore, Stoicism implores you to take responsibility for your happiness, not by seeking happiness from external gratification but by intrinsic happiness influenced by factors deep within you.

Happiness can only bloom from within if you fully take responsibility for breeding, watering, and watching it glow and grow. Embrace the things you can control and those within your reach. Stay away from external factors that are beyond your control. Things, factors, and influences beyond your control only increase worry, fear, and feelings of dissatisfaction.

Rise and take responsibility for your happiness. Grab every opportunity that makes your life fulfilling and your experiences satisfactory. Embrace every moment you have without worrying about what will happen later. Take comfort in the fact that we will all die and live a fulfilling life full of grace and happiness before that time comes.

Exercise to Change Your Perception

Almost all the renowned Stoics agree that life depends on how you perceive it. If you perceive it as challenging, then it will be challenging; if you perceive it as manageable and easy, then accept that reality, and it will be so.

The following is a good training exercise to help with the change of perception:

• **Zooming out to a cosmic or universal perspective.**

This is a technique often embraced by Marcus Aurelius. Whenever he felt challenged by the events of his life, he would look up to the sky, deeper into the stars, and imagine himself among them, journeying with them. That way, he would often change his perspective from personal to cosmic or universal.

You are being implored to employ the same technique in changing and shaping your perspective.

• Zooming in to overcome attachment to externals.

This technique is the opposite of zooming out. Instead of detaching from whatever you are attached to or whatever is bothering you, this technique helps you see the importance of not having to worry about certain things. For example, Marcus Aurelius often needed to seek validation from others, mainly regarding physical appearance.

However, the zooming-in technique made it easier to deal with such worries. The body is transient and will rot upon our deaths. Meditating about this and reminding yourself about it helps with the worry. This technique has been embraced across divides, including its use by Buddhist monks who meditate on images of rotting bodies to get rid of the urge to worry about physical appearances.

• Stretching time to see things from a long-term perspective.

Time always presents one with a better perspective. When you let time lapse and wait along before you react or take a step, chances are you are more likely to come up with a clear perspective that puts you in an excellent position to analyze and resolve your issues with clarity and finality. Time heals and allows you to take up a logical approach.

• Focus on the present moment.

Embracing the present allows you to hyper-focus on the events of the moment. It prevents you from focusing on the future or the past, which you have lost control over. Focusing on the present helps you handle each moment as it comes with the fullness of attention and passion. This makes your life much easier and more accommodating.

Do Less, Better

Aurelius on Focusing your Energy Wisely

Other Stoic philosophers, including Marcus Aurelius, have emphasized the principle of 'do less, better.' This principle's essence serves as a constructive reminder--to remind you of the obvious truth that a lot of energy and focus goes into doing more, but the results are hardly satisfactory. On the other hand, doing less comes with extremely good results.

This principle is a clarion call by Marcus Aurelius to himself and others to quit engaging in more just because it is possible. The perfect way to live a life of fulfillment and constant satisfaction is to do less to the best of your ability. When there is less to do, your energy is evenly and sufficiently distributed to ensure positive and progressive results.

The cry is for you to invest your time in the essential things; that time will take care of the rest. Taking on the essential few helps you attain excellence in what you do with little or no pressure.

How to Cut Out Inessential Activities

In his Meditations, Marcus Aurelius emphasizes doing less when one is overwhelmed. This, therefore, returns to the importance of cutting out inessentials and effectively managing this efficiency-promoting exercise.

The exercise of cutting out inessentials from amongst the things you do to increase your efficiency and productivity involves asking yourself a set of questions designed to sieve out the inessentials and leave you with the essentials that you can focus on or hyper-focus on to achieve high productivity.

The following are some of the riveting questions that you ought to ask yourself:

• What is essential?

This question will guide you in noting all the things and activities you need to engage in or do. After listing them, you eliminate those that are not essential based on urgency and importance. Therefore, your essential activities will roll back to important and urgent ones. This means they are of utmost value to the present moment and its fulfillment. In the end, it will facilitate the reduction of the things you can do.

• How can you focus on the process and not the result?

Focusing too much on the result could make you forget to emphasize the process. Failing to emphasize the process will eventually affect the results you keep focusing on. This means you have to focus on what is immediately before you.

• How can you enjoy what you have?

Wanting more eventually translates to greed, which drains joy. Therefore, it is significant to practice gratitude to ensure that you are content with what you have. When you are content with what you have, you cherish it, enjoy it, and adore it as much as possible because more is too much.

Death Is Knocking at Your Door

Aurelius on Memento Mori

'Memento mori' translates to "Remember you are going to die." This concept is embedded deep into Stoic philosophy. The essence of it all is to remind yourself often that you are not here forever. This is aimed at ensuring that you live your life with humility and take each moment as it comes. If you waste time in life, then you do not understand the concept of memento mori.

To great Stoics like Marcus Aurelius, the concept of Memento mori became a source of motivation and inspiration. Somehow, remembering that they could die anytime and that living life was not guaranteed made Marcus Aurelius live his life with gratitude.

He performed his role as a benevolent leader of Rome to the best of his ability, knowing he did not have forever. The same applies to you; you do not have forever. It is great to remember that you will die someday, and death is an event that is inevitable and a part of life. You are encouraged to live your life with contentment and practice gratitude to ensure you make the best of life.

How to Practice Memento Mori

The practice of Memento mori means living in gratitude. Remember that life is only a breath; be happy with your achievements. Do not feel sorry for yourself or regret because of how things went in the past. Additionally, do not worry yourself much about the future because, in the end, it is not yours to worry about. The universe decides what our collective and individual futures are. Death may very well be the future that the universe decides.

Negative Visualization

Negative visualization is a critical Stoic practice. This practice allows you to visualize misfortunes long in advance before they happen. This is important because it helps you deal with the anxiety that comes with the presence of misfortunes in one's life.

What happens is that you visualize or imagine a possible misfortune in your mind. The mind suffers all those anxieties and other effects during negative visualization. When the actual misfortune strikes, your mind interprets it as something it has already gone through, making mitigating the adverse effects and consequences and navigating through the misfortune easier.

The next chapter looks into modern-day Stoics--the people who keep this ancient practice and philosophy alive and well. They are the individuals who learned from the great Stoics of the past and took over the mantle of Stoic leadership, teaching, and practice.

Chapter 8

The New Stoics. A Look into the Contemporary Philosophers Shaping Today's Discourse

It is, after all, hard to know what to choose when you aren't really sure what you want. -William B Irvine

What Is Stoicism Today?

The world has indeed changed fundamentally. However, the practice of Stoicism has not changed much; the principles that guide and govern the philosophy in the contemporary world are the same principles that guided the philosophy during the times of Marcus Aurelius, Seneca, and Epictetus.

It is safe to say that the world has changed, but Stoicism still draws its power and strength from the past. Modern Stoics draw immense inspiration from the Stoics of the past. They embrace the philosophical practice just as much as the ancient philosophers did, the only difference being that times have truly changed.

Modern Practitioners of Ancient Wisdom

Today, many people around the world embrace Stoicism, an ancient philosophical approach to life. This philosophy teaches the importance of self-control, resilience, and clear thinking. Modern followers of Stoicism adopt its practices and principles, much like the great thinkers of ancient times did. These individuals uphold and celebrate the Stoic teachings, applying them to the challenges of contemporary life. Below are some examples of today's advocates who continue to spread this age-old wisdom:

Donald Robertson

Donald Robertson is a notable and rising figure in modern Stoicism. A psychotherapist by profession, Robertson has since found a unique blend of Stoicism and psychology. He has formulated methods that link the ancient practice of Stoicism with mental resilience. Robertson was right in his findings; the essence of Stoicism, even in ancient times, was to foster resilience in the individuals who embraced it.

This unique finding by Robertson can be identified and found in probably all individuals in the circle of the ancient philosophers. Remember how Marcus Aurelius won wars and went to war for Rome without ever losing his mental composure or how Epictetus went through slavery and came out stronger and more successful? These stories can inspire such a finding as the one by Donald Robertson. In addition, people in the contemporary world have gotten into Stoicism to grow resilient to the problems and challenges of the contemporary world.

His magnificent publication in the form of a book called "Stoicism and the Art of Happiness" has not failed in making Stoicism a worthwhile endeavor. It pursues the Stoic principle of Eudaemonia, which translates to happiness. Every individual in the modern world is interested in the pursuit of happiness despite the massive challenges that bedevil our world. The pursuit of happiness remains a noble adventure for most individuals, and Donald Robertson has taken advantage of human beings' inclination to showcase the essence of embracing and practicing Stoicism.

Donald Robertson Quotes

Some of the quotes from Donald Robertson in his works are as follows:

"To learn how to die, according to the Stoics, is to unlearn how to be a slave."

In this quote, Robertson implies that as a human being, you are attached to the intricacies of life. However, this attachment to the various intricacies of life is a form of slavery in itself. Therefore, the earlier you learn not to attach yourself, the more you are unlearning how to be a slave and, therefore, accept that at the end of life, there is death, and the excessive attachment to the intricacies of this life is not very necessary.

"From the moment we were born, we are constantly dying, not only with each stage of life but also one day at a time. As Marcus put it, our bodies are not the ones our mothers gave birth to. Nobody is the same as he was yesterday. Realizing this makes it easier to let go; we can no more hold on to life than grasp the waters of a rushing stream."

Through this quote, Robertson implores you to embrace the fleeting nature of life. Life is a journey, and each day is different. The events and obstacles are different. Even our bodies are constantly giving up life with each passing day. This is a reminder that life is nothing but a temporary adventure. There is a need to detach from its intricacies, especially those that have passed us. The true essence of life is to focus on the present moment because that is where the secret of life is.

In his works, Donald Robertson has left us with numerous mind-boggling and life-shaping quotes with magnificent learning lessons. His works have been briefly highlighted as follows:

The Works of Donald Robertson

How to Think Like a Roman Emperor: The Stoic Philosophy of Marcus Aurelius

With this publication, Robertson once again takes us through the journey of Stoicism through the life and works of Marcus Aurelius. We are all acquainted with the works of Marcus Aurelius by now. However, Donald Robertson looks at the life and works of Emperor Marcus Aurelius from a unique perspective.

This publication emphasizes the importance of living and embracing a virtuous life, just as the ancient Stoic Marcus Aurelius did, particularly considering contemporary life.

In this book, Donald Robertson, apart from taking us through the unique journey of Rome's good emperor, creates a unique blend between Stoicism and Cognitive Behavioral Therapy (CBT) because he is a Psychotherapist by profession. This unique blend essentially forms a part of the modern version of Stoicism, making it suitable to guide us in tackling contemporary world problems, drawing immense inspiration from men as great as Marcus Aurelius.

In the end, this book emphasizes living a life guided by virtue. Among the Stoic virtues often impressed upon, Donald Robertson sheds specific light on the tremendous Stoic virtue of Resilience in this book.

Stoicism and the Art of Happiness: Practical Wisdom for Everyday Life.

This is yet another splendid attempt by Donald Robertson to bring the ancient wisdom of Stoic Philosophy to the modern world. The book categorically presents an armamentarium of Stoic-inspired strategies for pursuing happiness in modern life.

Donald Robertson once again demonstrates the essence of resilience in the pursuit of life's happiness in the chapters of this book. Further into the chapters, he emphasizes the importance of living in harmony with nature and the ways of the universe. Harmony with nature and cosmic or universal providence is the way to happiness. He implores all individuals to go through life knowing and accepting that nature provides what it wants, when it wants, and how it wants, and can take it away just the same.

Therefore, true happiness lies in understanding, accepting, and embracing the ways of nature just as they are. Find a harmonious way of existing with nature and the universal cum cosmic impact on our lives, and you will see life's happiness. The ancient Stoics believed in this, which is what the modern Stoics should embrace.

The Philosophy of Cognitive Behavioral Therapy(CBT): Stoic Philosophy as Rational and Cognitive Psychotherapy

Donald Robertson explores the intricate links between psychotherapy and Socratic philosophies like Stoicism in this book. He indicates that Stoicism provided the basis for psychotherapy.

The book provides techniques that blend psychotherapy and Stoicism. It further discusses the effect of rationality, a Stoic philosophy concept, on psychotherapy. In the end, Donald Robertson gives us a unique account of how important Stoicism is to Cognitive Behavioral Therapy (CBT) and how one can incorporate this unique blend into one's way of life.

William B. Irvine

William B. Irvine confesses to having embraced the practice of Stoicism as a way to prepare himself for old age. Undoubtedly, he knew old age would come with its challenges, challenges he had never encountered before. As a young person, Irvine had never really faced many health challenges. He once suffered from Pneumonia, from which he recovered and never contracted it again. He recounts not suffering any illness for the next few decades after his Pneumonia ordeal.

However, his old age years, or early old age, as Irvine refers to them, have not been as smooth as his younger years. Nothing is the same, and it took him a while to acknowledge that old age means precisely that. You can not be old and young at the same time. Your biological composition would prove different.

Irvine embraces stoicism to tackle life from a rational point of view. He knew that growing old, he needed a mind shift; therefore, at fifty, he adopted Stoicism as a way of life. Seventeen years later, he discovered how important that choice to practice Stoicism had been. He still felt young and strong at fifty, and so did many people. He would even be sure to go for medical checkups as a formality.

At sixty-seven years of age, however, medical checkups were no longer a matter of formal disposition to tick a box; they became necessary. He would develop a slight complication here or an arm dislocation there; these are the things that old age brought to his life. Stoicism is his way of getting through the challenges of old age, and in return, William B. Irvine is now one of the revered modern Stoics even after embracing the practice later in his life.

Famous Quotes by William B. Irvine

The following are some of William B. Irvine's best quotes for personal reflection:

"We humans are largely unhappy because we are insatiable. After working hard to get what we want, we routinely lose interest in the object of our desire. Rather than feeling satisfied, we feel a bit bored, and in response to this boredom, we form new, even grander desires."

In this quote, Irvine addresses the insatiable nature of human desire. The point here is that there is no end to desire; if anything, the supposed end of a particular desire is the beginning of a new one, which could be even bigger than the first one. The lesson from these words by William B. Irvine is that a life without desires is a much more satisfactory life than one riddled by desire because desire never really ends.

"The problem is that bad men obey their lusts as servants obey their masters, and because they cannot control their desires, they can never find contentment."

Here, William B. Irvine addresses the impact of lustful desires on an individual's life. Lust is like a master; when you heed it, you become its servant with no control over your life. The lesson is that lust can never be fulfilled. The moment you give in, the more you will want. The secret is not to heed lust but to observe restraint and embrace virtue.

"Stoicism, understood properly, is a cure for a disease. The disease in question is the anxiety, grief, fear, and various other negative emotions that plague humans and prevent them from experiencing a joyful existence."

Irvine uses this quote to showcase the true importance of Stoicism in mitigating anxiety and its effects. In the end, it is a well-known fact that most anxiety stems from constant worry about the future or even the past. Stoicism advocates for seizing the moment, living each moment as it comes. As a Stoic, the past, future, or even what others think about you are external factors beyond your control. There is, therefore, no point in fixating upon such matters as they will only add to your anxiety and constantly subtract from your peace of mind and mental composure.

"Around the world and throughout the millennia, those who have thought carefully about the workings of desire have recognized that the easiest way for us to gain happiness is to learn how to want the things we already have."

Again, Irvine takes this opportunity to implore us to love what we already have and abandon the desire for more. Loving what you already have makes it easy not to desire more. The rationale here is that if you have already embraced what you have as enough, you will have no desire for things you do not have. They would not be meaningful to you anyway. Therefore, the significance of fully accepting, embracing, and being content with what you already have cannot be understated.

The Works of William B. Irvine

The following are some of the great works of William B. Irvine:

A Guide to the Good Life: The Ancient Art of Stoic Joy

In this book, Irvine illuminates various aspects, among them the tragedy of having no philosophy. He emphasizes that philosophy gives purpose. In essence, William B. Irvine impresses here that if you believe in nothing, you stand for nothing.

He further touches on negative visualization, the dichotomy of control, and hedonic adaptation. On negative visualization, he says it prepares an individual for the worst-case scenario, therefore leaving no room for anxiety and worry. On the dichotomy of control, he implores us to focus on the internal factors within our control, let alone external factors that are not within our purview.

In the hedonic adaptation, he uses the scenario of a lottery winner to provide context. What he brings out is the fact that you can desire something grander than what you have, like is the case of lottery winners who, after winning and purchasing fancy cars or even houses, will reach a certain point and start taking their new acquisitions for granted the same way they took for granted what they had before winning the lottery. This eventually rolls back to the desire for more, which, in essence, is greed.

The Stoic Challenge: A Philosopher's Guide to Becoming Calmer, Tougher, and More Resilient

This book is tailored to guide you through dealing with challenges. Essentially, it summarizes Stoicism's approach to dealing with things we cannot control. Throughout the chapters, the message is the importance of using internal factors, or rather, the things that we can control, to triumph through the difficult times created by external factors, the things we cannot control.

The Works of Ryan Holiday

The following are the great works of Ryan Holiday that are based on Stoic Philosophy:

The Daily Stoic: 366 Meditations on Wisdom, Perseverance, and the Art of Living

In this book, Ryan Holiday introduces habits and daily practices that can foster the growth of a Stoic. The emphasis is on wisdom, perseverance, and the art of living, as Holiday calls it.

The book curates Stoic-inspired words of wisdom, Stoic practices, and habits that you would embrace to transform your life and become a Stoic. Some of the habits and practices that Irvine considers in this book include self-examination and constantly reassessing the kind of people you associate yourself with. Often, the people you associate with impact your life more than you would naturally estimate or appreciate.

The Obstacle is the Way: The Timeless Art of Turning Trials into Triumphs

The primary focus of this book is on turning obstacles around. Generally, obstacles are meant to derail us from our purpose, goals, aims, and aspirations. The story becomes utterly different when we turn these obstacles into opportunities. Can you turn an obstacle into an opportunity? That is the question that Ryan Holiday tries to answer in this book.

Indeed, obstacles can be turned into opportunities. However, this process requires you to take the primary step of ignoring what is beyond your control or external seconds. The second step is to focus on what you can control. Identify all the factors you can control and use them to your advantage.

The book, in short, tries to convey the message that those who remain steadfast in their pursuit of purpose can at least turn obstacles into triumphs. If you waiver from your purpose, your target, or your goal, it becomes easier for the challenge to take you over. Challenges are, therefore, opportunities waiting to be turned around.

Ego is the Enemy: The Fight to Master our Greatest Opponent

Ego is our greatest opponent, and words can never be truer than these. This is the message in this book. Ryan Holiday points out the various effects of ego on one's life, but he does not stop there. He goes further and pinpoints viable strategies to deal with ego. Ego is normal, but being average is no license to prevent one from diligently achieving one's goals and aspirations or, at the very least, living one's life in harmony with the universe and cosmic providence.

Holiday emphasizes that ego is an unhealthy belief in your importance. This enemy, ego, has the following effects on your life, as brought out by Holiday in this book: Losing sight of reality and doing less but talking more. The crucial lessons that you would pick from this book are laced with thematic topics that Holiday uses to drive his point home, and they are as follows: Live with a purpose as opposed to passion, always keep learning, do more, and talk less. These valuable lessons would go a long way in facilitating the defeat of ego as an enemy.

Stillness is the Key: An Ancient Strategy for Modern Life

In this book, Ryan Holiday implores us to embrace the timeless trinity of mind, body, and soul. In brief, about the mind, Ryan Holiday says to focus on today, avoid ego, and journal. Focusing on other moments from the present is futile and damaging. The only moment you are in control of is the present moment. The ego is our biggest enemy as human beings and does more harm than good. Therefore, avoiding it proves more advantageous to our well-being. Journaling is a meditative exercise that helps strengthen the mind, eliminate overwhelming things, and embrace your situation.

Regarding the soul or spirit, Ryan Holiday focuses on choosing virtue over everything else, contentment, and living in harmony with nature. On virtue, there is no doubt that Stoicism prides itself on virtuous living. Holiday demonstrates virtue as soothing for the soul and a virtuous life as a fulfilling and happiness-creating life. On contentment, he implores us to learn to say enough. Be content with what you have to avoid the unnecessary desire for more and more, which will, in the end, negatively impact your life by giving you unnecessary anxiety. Living in harmony with nature requires that you accept nature's providence as it is. In the end, the most important lesson is that we are not in control of the events of life, that is the universe's work.

Finally, on the body, this is the vessel that carries you through life. It also houses your mind and plays home for your soul. Enjoy leisure, enjoy your hobbies, and walk here and there. Do things and activities that facilitate the health and well-being of your body.

Courage is Calling: Fortune Favors the Brave

In this book, Ryan Holiday sheds light on the importance of courage. As a Stoic pillar and virtue, courage does not mean the absence of fear. Instead, it is the taking of logical action despite fear. Remember, Stoicism is not about eliminating or depressing emotions but rationalizing them. Therefore, what courage does is rationalize fear, which then allows you to act from a logical point of view, even in difficult times.

He also emphasizes that courage is not an impulse but rather a result of repeated preparation. Often, those who act out of courage are said to be impulsive. That is not the case. They have prepared for the situation in which they act to the extent that the fear in them that would have stopped them from acting has been rationalized, making it easier to act.

He defines courage as not being afraid to act even when others are afraid to act. It is acting when others are too scared to do that separates the courageous from those who are not.

Massimo Pigliucci

Pigliucci is an author and professor of Philosophy at City College in New York. He is one of the most prolific proponents of Stoicism in the contemporary world. He has published books on Stoic philosophy, in which he provides guidelines and insights on incorporating Stoicism into modern life.

Quotes by Massimo Pigliucci

"One of the first lessons from Stoicism, then, is to focus our attention and efforts where we have the most power and let the universe run as it will. This will save us both a lot of energy and worry".

This quote by Pigliucci is inspired by the Stoic principle of living in the present and living in harmony with nature and nature's providence. All external factors are beyond our control--either they are in the control of other people, the universe, or a supernatural being. Therefore, it does not do us well to focus our attention where we have no power. It comes down to focusing on our inner selves, where our power lies.

"Now there are three stages of wisdom: the unwise person blames others for what are, in the end, her judgments about things; the person making progress does not blame others, but only herself; the wise do not blame even herself."

Massimo Pigliucci reveals that you can not blame others or yourself through this quote. One of the pillars of Stoicism is wisdom, which requires that you live in the present. Blame is anchored in past frustrations; therefore, in Stoic balance, it is unacceptable.

"Shaping your character is ultimately the only thing under your control."

This quote is also anchored on the Stoic teaching of focusing on internal factors- the things we can control- instead of external factors beyond our control. Character is shaped from within, and by Stoic standards, character is shaped through virtuous living. Therefore, Pigliucci implores us to shape our lives from within because that is where we have complete control.

The Works of Massimo Pigliucci

The following are the works of Massimo Pigliucci in summary:

A Handbook for New Stoics

Massimo Pigliucci echoes the age-old Stoic teaching of embracing virtue in this book. He showcases the interconnection between Stoic virtuous living and happiness. Virtuous living puts you in control of your life. Your actions are pure and in harmony with nature, therefore leaving less room for regrets.

Massimo Pigliucci goes further to introduce the other core principles of Stoicism. At this point, he focuses on the dichotomy of control. We should focus on things within our control, leading us to shape and mold our inner selves the Stoic way.

How to Be a Stoic

Massimo Pigliucci organizes this book as a discussion between himself and the great Stoic philosopher Epictetus. This gives it an entertaining touch that captivates the reader while delivering the message in its best form.

The key takeaways in this book are: Some things are within our power while others are not. This is a lesson that Stoic Philosophy has emphasized since time immemorial. It is good to focus on the things that are within our control and disregard those that are not. The other key takeaway is to live life in harmony with nature. Our lives depend on nature's providence; we can not dictate the course of nature because we have no control over it. Therefore, the best bet is to live in harmony with nature and accept and embrace nature's providence. Going against nature often proves to be a futile exercise.

Finally, he talks about using spiritual exercises to beat the odds. Here, Pigliucci reminds us that eventually, Stoicism starts being a spiritual exercise, and as a student of Stoicism, it reaches a point where the note-taking and writing ends. When you graduate to a spiritual Stoic, you embody the philosophy in all your doings and practice it in every aspect of your life, including trivial or minor disagreements with family or friends.

How to Live a Good Life

In this book, Pigliucci draws inspiration from Buddhism. His focus is on ethical living; essentially, he sets out to answer the question of what ethical living is. He defines ethical living as a way of life in which one tries as much as possible to reduce the hurt or evil in the world. This means one tries to act ethically and calmly.

The key takeaway is the Dalai Lama's response to the question of whether killing Hitler would be an ethical thing. The Dalai Lama consults with other spiritual leaders and responds that it would be ethical only if you do not get angry. This means that you did the killing calmly and rationally to reduce the harm in the world. Therefore, this gives insight into the fact that ethical living is living a life that positively contributes to the general good. These are teachings that are echoed through Stoic philosophy as well.

A Field Guide to a Happy Life

This book is curated as a guideline for achieving enlightened serenity. The emphasis is on living life as it is, not what we wish it to be. Pigluicci incorporates modern science approaches into Stoicism to make it more modern-friendly and easy to relate to.

Pigluicci further emphasizes the importance of controlling our judgments and adopted values. These things stem from our inner selves and are within our control. He impresses us and helps us understand that nothing else is within our control.

The next chapter focuses on embracing Stoicism in our daily lives and incorporating it into our actions. The essence of doing this has been showcased in the current chapter and will be further delved into in the next one.

Chapter 9

Embracing Stoicism in Everyday Life

Well-being is realized in small steps, but it is truly no small thing. -Zeno

On Consistency

To be consistent refers to maintaining a particular way of doing things even as the surrounding circumstances change. Consistency is not limited to a way of doing things but also the quality of your work.

Consistency has, therefore, been recognized by both Stoics and non-Stoics as one of the best and most reliable ways of attaining success. When you are consistent, you can make progress effortlessly because each day you work on your tasks, yourself, or your goals, there are high chances of improvement, as opposed to when you are not consistent with your goals or achievements.

In Stoic philosophical parlance, consistency helps you excel in your Stoic practice. Without consistency in Stoicism, you are likely to fall out of following this great way of life. It is, therefore, significant that you embrace consistency in your Stoic way of life.

For instance, if you start living a virtuous life, as Stoicism requires, it is prudent to do it consistently; this is the only way you will enjoy the fruits of Stoicism. Consistency breeds success and progress; it keeps you grounded on your goals, achievements, and even a philosophical way of life like Stoicism.

The following are some of the benefits of consistency:

• Inspires a positive reputation.

When you are consistent, your reliability and trustworthiness increase. It is easier to trust someone who consistently works on themselves, their goals, and their achievements as opposed to someone who shows up for their goals and achievements once in a while or during moments of convenience and then disappears.

• Builds self-confidence.

The more you consistently work on yourself and your goals, the more confidence you start developing in yourself and your abilities. Consistency delivers for you and builds your confidence gradually with each passing day. When you are inconsistent, it is improbable that you will make any progress regarding your confidence.

• Helps distinguish what is essential and what is not.

Your focus is narrowed down to essential things when you are consistent with your goals. In essence, consistency helps you bring out the essential things. When you are inconsistent, everything goes since you are not committed to a specific focus.

• It strengthens resolve and determination.

Consistent resolve and determination keep strengthening because you develop stronger muscles for your goals and way of life. You master what you do and want to do more of it despite the circumstances.

• It fosters patience.

The virtue of patience is a hard bargain and sometimes even a hard sell. However, when you are consistent, you subconsciously develop the virtue of patience. You no longer need to sell yourself to the idea or convince yourself in favor of patience. What will happen is that with your consistent actions, you grow patient. Today, consistency is a breeding ground for the virtue of patience.

On Good Habits

Good habits are the glue that binds you to your Stoic nature and life. They are progressive and positive and facilitate the common good in one way or another. Bad habits, on the other hand, are harmful and not in favor of the common good. In the end, the common good is what Stoicism advocates. Habits form the very fabric of our lives, and the good ones propel us forward toward our goals and the achievement of a fulfilling life.

The following are the benefits of good habits:

• **Good habits facilitate the replacement of bad habits.**

Good habits are often the only viable antidote for bad habits. Counter every bad habit with a good habit and focus on the good one. It will eventually neutralize, outshine, and replace the bad habit.

• **They increase your overall quality of life.**

Good habits are harbingers of a good life. Nothing positive manifests negativity. Therefore, by embracing good habits, you are manifesting a good and quality life. This will come through the gradual process of improvement.

• **Good habits help you reach your goals.**

Good habits are valuable tools for pursuing and reaching your goals. Therefore, incorporating good habits into your life makes it easier to attain your goals. Good habits help you develop a sense of discipline. It is the discipline that facilitates the consistent pursuit of your goals.

Think Small

How to Build Small Micro Habits That Stick

We often fixate on making instant progress; motivational speakers have fueled this urge. This notion of instant progress is, however, based on willpower. Willpower, however, acts like a muscle; one moment, it is strong, and the next moment, perhaps even on impulse, it's relaxed. Therefore, as it is, willpower lacks the consistency to facilitate that lasting change that we require. Stoicism broadly advocates for the development of micro habits to foster lasting change. The significance of micro habits cannot be understated. They are powerful tools that can turn your life around in immeasurable ways.

How do we develop these micro habits that foster lasting change?

The following are some of the strategies you can take on to build on micro habits that stick:

• Start with one habit at a time.

Habits are often a hard bargain to develop, and you cannot honestly be blamed for being unable to develop one. Therefore, it is reasonable that when you want to develop a habit or a set of habits, you at least start with one. This makes it easier to follow through and make progress. Developing numerous habits will become a cumbersome and eventually overwhelming exercise.

• Have everything you need at hand.

Ensuring you have every tool or equipment that you need or will potentially need to facilitate the development of a habit is an essential step. Often, when you are developing a new habit, you need to be fully engaged in or tenants of that development; therefore, eliminating possible barriers makes your work easier. If you need your phone or a particular device, it is essential to ensure it is fully available and accessible to make your habit development exercise hassle-free.

• Incorporate new habits into existing ones.

New habits might be difficult to start or even follow through due to their obvious lack of familiarity. However, it becomes much easier when you incorporate such new habits into your old habits. Incorporating or blending new habits with old ones gives them the familiarity you need to be comfortable adopting them into your daily routine and eventually turning them into independent habits.

Good Micro Habits to Start With

It is essential not only to develop your micro habits but also to make sure they are good ones. Developing bad habits is destructive and contrary to the spirit and nature of Stoicism and your well-being. The following are some of the good micro habits that you can build upon:

• If you want to make a significant investment, make small weekly or monthly investments, depending on your preference. They eventually become a significant investment.

• Start scheduling your next day a day beforehand so that you have time to prepare and do the things you have planned when that day comes.• Break your long-term goals into achievable daily goals and begin ticking them off individually. This will make it easier for you to develop the discipline of constantly chasing your goals and even achieving those that may seem complex in the long run.

• When the day comes for daybreak, tidy your desk up to ensure that the next day does not start with the gruesome task of arranging and rearranging things before you get into the day's activities.

• To clear your mind, listen to a thought-provoking podcast, walk, or drink.

• Always try to remove all distractions from your place of work before you begin to work.

Create a Routine

The objective truth behind the noble practice of routine creation is that it helps individuals develop a sense of discipline and commitment to their work, whether it be small achievements and tasks or life-altering ones.

How to Build a Routine and Stick to It

The following are some of the strategies to consider in building a new routine:

To begin with, decide what you want to include in your routine. This is important in ensuring that you prioritize the things that are important to you, your goals, and your well-being.

The next step is to lay out a plan for your routine. As an aspiring Stoic, a routine fosters discipline and consistency. In this step, ask yourself what you want to do, at what time, and where. These important questions will guide the plan you create for your routine.

If you want your routine to work for you, then you should be consistent with your time. It is the consistency that will inspire the discipline that you will require to be able to stick to your routine. Therefore, be as consistent as possible with the time allocations in your routine.

It is also essential to make your routine fun. Life is too short and unpredictable to engage in things that are boring and draining at the same time. Making your routine fun by all means necessary gives it the exciting and enticing nature that would foster a curious commitment in you to look forward to keeping that routine or, at the very least, exploring it.

After you have worked on your routine, it is necessary to track your progress. After all, the essence of even having a routine in the first place is for personal or even professional improvement. Devising a method or system to track your progress is the best way to ensure you are working towards and in favor of that improvement, not vice versa.

Setting up a Morning Routine

Stoic Morning Routine Habit Suggestions

It is no secret that almost every proponent of Stoicism has implored you to embrace Stoicim and incorporate it into your life to turn it around. True to that, Stoicism is a great life philosophy, and its practice is life-changing and for the better. However, how do you incorporate stoicism into your daily life? One way is through Stoic morning routine habits. The following are some of the Stoic suggestions for your morning routine:

• **Mindfulness meditation.**

Stoicism emphasizes the power of the mind and describes the mind as the only factor within our control. Therefore, mindfulness meditation is not only a common Stoic technique but also one of the most widely practiced techniques by both practitioners and non-practitioners of Stoicism. This tells you that this technique's reputation precedes it.

During your mindfulness meditation, which also doubles as your mindful watch, reflect on the virtues you will want to embrace during the day. Ask yourself how you will make it possible to practice those virtues. Then, go on and start the activities of the day, bearing in mind what you have just reflected on and your resolution after the personal reflection.

• **Practice gratitude.**

Each morning, as you wake up and experience the shining sun and the birds singing in rejoicing to the universal providence that has been availed to them, join them in offering gratitude. Be as grateful as the birds of the air for the providence God or the universe provides.

Be grateful for all your things and opportunities, knowing that perhaps you are not the only person deserving of such good things; someone else is, too. Acknowledging that you are no more special than the next or last person ensures you maintain humility and gratitude for the good graces.

Gratitude also fosters positivity in your demeanor, conduct, and life. Positivity ensures you can turn even the most difficult tasks around. A person with positivity will always find a way to settle challenges without excuses. It is excellent to aspire to be grateful at all times of your life, no matter your circumstances.

End Each Day Constructively

Stoic Night Routine Habit Suggestions

Often, we emphasize how we start our day because no one wants to have a bad day. Everybody would prefer a calm or positively exciting day. Therefore, we put much of our preparation and mindfulness into starting the day instead of finishing the day. However, Stoicism indicates that finishing the day on a good note matters just the same. To facilitate finishing your day on a good note and having a Stoic evening, here is an amazing three-part routine for a decent Stoic evening:

• **Journal review.**

Both Seneca and Epictetus have emphasized the importance of night journaling. They say you should not sleep without contemplating and soul-searching your activities of the day. They implore you to sit down with yourself and your thoughts and make good use of your journal.

Ask yourself the most important questions of the day. Where did you go wrong? What can you do to avoid such a situation? Were your activities of the day virtuous and in service of the common good?

These questions will help you examine how you conducted yourself during the day and what you can do to rectify the situation. The essence of this exercise is mindfulness and self-improvement to ensure you do not repeat the same errors. It helps you improve each day.

• Meditation.

The benefits of meditation are widely acclaimed and well-known. It brings clarity, focus, and calmness of mind. Therefore, as you wind up your day and settle into the dark night after a long and active day, settle down for a few minutes of meditation to refocus and recenter your mind as you look forward to a new day and the providence of the universe.

• Contemplation of finality.

Contemplation is the last part of the day. It helps you finish your day with satisfaction, knowing that you have done everything you set out to do. As you lay yourself to rest, you do so with a calm and collected mind. It helps you look forward to the next day, knowing that you have done all you could as diligently as you could.

Give Yourself the Order to Quit

How to Know When to Quit

Often, quitting is looked down upon as being weak or giving up. However, in Stoic parlance, there is no such thing as giving up, and quitting is certainly not considered a weak move. In Stoicism, quitting is simply resigning to the will of the universe. Some things come to you by universal providence; you have no control over them and will never have control over them. Therefore, for those things that rely on universal providence, no matter how badly you want them to be yours, the universe might assign them to you.

Therefore, since such things are precisely beyond your control, you must teach yourself to resign and surrender to universal providence. When you try to chase something, and somehow you cannot get it, surrender to the will of the universe and pray that the universe will be kind to you. Even if it is not, still be grateful that you have what you have.

How to Break Bad Habits

Bad habits often cause pain in most people's necks. You can find yourself beating yourself up and clouding yourself with judgment and emotion because of certain bad habits you may have knowingly or unknowingly incorporated into your life. Suddenly, you realize they are habits you need to get rid of, but you may be facing one problem or another.

Here are some of the methods you can practice to break bad habits.

The most critical step in breaking a habit is identifying the trigger moments. What time of the day is that habit triggered? What triggers that habit? The instant you identify the times in which your habits are triggered and what triggers them, begin the journey of avoiding those triggers and trigger moments. Additionally, you can replace the habit with a new one.

How to Motivate Yourself to Do Something Difficult

Life will always hit you with things that you will find difficult. However, the spirit of Stoicism is not for avoiding difficulties but embracing them. Difficult does not mean impossible; if it is not, then it can be done. The following are some of the ways you can bring yourself around to do those things that you often find difficult:

• Have a clear goal in mind.

When you set a clear goal, that goal becomes your driving force; it propels you past all the difficulties. It becomes all that matters, and all the obstacles that may stand in your way become the way. Therefore, it helps a great deal to have a clear goal in mind. Whatever you're going after, let it be a clear goal you can commit to, no matter the circumstances.

• Consider having an accountability partner.

You often hear of romantic partners, and that's beautiful; however, having an accountability partner is even more interesting. You know that person you can always count on to call you out whenever you want to give up just because you are facing a difficulty or two. This must be a person who understands both you and the nature of your goals.

• Associate yourself with people who make you better.

Better make for better, not worse. Therefore, as you go about your life and encounter various challenges, ensure that you associate yourself with people who sharpen you--individuals who brighten your life as much as they brighten you. They inspire you as much as they help you learn and tackle life's difficulties. Dissociate from the miserable.

Overcoming the Fear of Change

It has been an established universal truth that change is the only constant in life. No matter how much you hate it or how averse you may be to change, it will still come. Most people hate change because it comes with a certain unpredictability. Human nature nurtures the fear of the unknown; change is often the unknown.

Do not let the fear of the unknown control you. Do not let it stop you from embracing change because change is inevitable. If you don't embrace it, it will still come, and you will be at a disadvantage. Let change find you welcoming and adaptable to it; that is the spirit of Stoicism echoed by the likes of Marcus Aurelius, Epictetus, Seneca, and even modern Stoics like Donald Robertson. That is the message they try to convey in their numerous teachings on resilience as Stoics.

Listen Before You Speak

Listening is an essential tool, especially in Stoicism. Stoicism advocates for reacting to things or occurrences logically instead of emotionally because you must listen and understand to employ logic. Emotionally, you can react without thinking through anything or even evaluating everything. You are, therefore, implored to listen carefully and often before you speak. Listening will allow you to absorb as much information as you require to take a logical step. Suffice it to say that listening removes the chances of an emotional reaction.

The following are some of the approaches to use to ensure that you always listen before you speak:

• **Always remember that silence is golden.**

Whenever you listen to another person speak, let them finish what they intend to say. Even when they pause midway, it does not mean they are done. Just maintain silence until they finish. That is the only way you can get complete information and clearly indicate what they meant to say.

• **You do not have to fix it, react immediately, or even react at all.**

You do not have to react even when the person you are listening to is done talking. You can still opt to remain silent and give yourself more time to process the information or even find a logical approach and response.

• You do not have to win.

Stoicism teaches that the true goal of listening isn't to prepare a counterargument or to secure a personal victory. Rather, it is genuinely comprehending and making logical sense of what is being said. Effective listening means engaging with the ideas presented, analyzing them for their logical consistency, and considering how they can contribute to the common good. In this way, listening becomes a thoughtful act aimed at understanding and wisdom rather than merely an opportunity to assert one's own views.

Conclusion

As we close the curtain on our exploration of Stoicism, let us reflect on the profound journey we have embarked upon together. "The Triad of Stoicism" has not merely been a study of ancient texts or philosophical discourses; it has been a call to action--a vibrant invitation to embody the virtues that have withstood the tumult of centuries.

In the pages of this book, we have traversed the pathways walked by the great Stoic philosophers, uncovering the timeless principles of wisdom, courage, and moderation. We have seen how these principles are not relics of a bygone era but are beacons that light our way in the modern world. They offer solace in our struggles, clarity in our chaos, and resilience in our recoveries.

Stoicism teaches us that the essence of a fulfilled life does not lie in the external accolades or material possessions we accumulate but in the strength of our character and the quality of our actions. It challenges us to look within, refine our intentions, and act with purpose and integrity, no matter the storms we face.

As you set down this book, remember that the journey of Stoicism does not end here. It is a continuous quest for growth and understanding. Each day offers a new opportunity to practice restraint, embrace challenges as opportunities for development, and extend kindness and justice in our interactions.

Let the Triad of Stoicism--wisdom, courage, and moderation--be your guiding stars. Carry forward the torch of this ancient wisdom, not just as a philosophy to ponder but as a way of life to live passionately and profoundly. In the words of Marcus Aurelius, "Waste no more time arguing about what a good man should be. Be one."

Thus, armed with the knowledge and virtues of the Stoics, step boldly into the arena of life. Transform obstacles into stepping stones and forge a legacy of resilience and virtue. This is the heart of Stoic living, and it is within your power to live it every day.

With every breath and action, let us rekindle the spirit of the Stoics, for in their wisdom lies the key to enduring life's challenges and thriving among them. The echoes of Stoic wisdom are not whispers from the past; they are the roaring winds that propel us forward into a future of possibility and purpose.

Embrace the triad, live their philosophy, and become the architect of your own fate. This is the essence of Stoicism, and now it is yours to claim.

With Stoicism, your life becomes more accessible, and it is not just because Stoicism teaches the essence and practice of resilience but also because Stoicism shapes you to be disciplined and embrace adversity.

When you embrace virtuous living, you can embrace what nature gives you, positive or negative, until nature decides to elevate you or bring your day of rest closer.

Congratulations & Thank You!

Wow, you've done it! You've journeyed through the "THE TRIAD OF STOICISM" pages and walked the path alongside Marcus Aurelius, Seneca, and Epictetus. I hope their wisdom has enlightened you and empowered you to embrace a more stoic, serene approach to life's twists and turns.

Now, I have a small favor to ask—and yes, it involves a little more of your time, but in the best way possible!

Could you share your thoughts? Your feedback is invaluable, not just to me but also to future readers navigating their own paths toward inner peace and resilience. Your insights could light the way for someone else looking for guidance in this hectic world. Plus, it's always wonderful to connect with readers who are on the same journey!

Choyo Gomex

To leave your feedback:

1. Open your camera app.
2. Point your mobile device at the QR code below.
3. The review page will appear in your web browser.

Or visit: https://www.amazon.com/dp/B0DQKKNHTT

Thank you!

Plus, a little bit of good karma:

Sharing your review is like sending out a ripple of positivity. It's about putting something good into the universe that will hopefully circle back to you. Plus, who doesn't like to see their name and thoughts influencing others positively?

Thank you once again for reading "THE TRIAD OF STOICISM." It was a pleasure sharing this journey with you, and I hope the teachings of these great philosophers continue to inspire and guide you every day.

Ready to make a difference? It's review time!

Your words can inspire the next wave of readers and bring more stoic wisdom into their lives. Thank you for being such an essential part of this philosophical journey!

Hello Enlightened Reader,

Congratulations on completing "THE TRIAD OF STOICISM: *Using the Ancient Teachings of Marcus Aurelius, Seneca & Epictetus to Cultivate Inner Peace."*

You've embarked on a profound journey, delving into the timeless wisdom of Stoic philosophers to gain deeper insight into the self and cultivate lasting inner peace. Your dedication to understanding and applying these ancient teachings is truly commendable.

As a special thank you for your commitment to personal growth, I'm offering you an exclusive 45-minute one-on-one personalized coaching session via Zoom at no cost to you.

This is an opportunity to explore any aspect of Stoic wisdom or other topics related to self-mastery and inner peace, guided by my expertise as a Master NLP Practitioner trained by Dr. Richard Bandler.

To claim your session, email me at choyo@gomex.com with the subject line "Next Level Inner Peace," and we'll find a time that works for you.

Thank you for your dedication to cultivating a peaceful and centered life. I look forward to supporting you further on your journey to true serenity.

Wishing you continued peace and wisdom,

Choyo Gomex

References

"30 Best Seneca Quotes with Image | Bookey." Www.bookey.app, www.bookey.app/quote-author/seneca. Accessed 6 Apr. 2024.

Allan. "What Is Stoic Eudaimonia?" What Is Stoicism?, 27 Nov. 2022, whatisstoicism.com/stoicism-definition/what-is-stoic-eudaimonia/.

Dedes, Ioannis. "Seneca the Younger: 10 Stoic Quotes for Valuable Life Advice Curiosmos." Curiosmos.com, 13 Apr. 2022, curiosmos.com/seneca-the-younger-10-stoic-quotes-for-valuable-life-advice/. Accessed 6 Apr. 2024.

Gotter, Ana. "8 Breathing Exercises to Try When You Feel Anxious." Healthline, 22 Apr. 2019, www.healthline.com/health/breathing-exercises-for-anxiety.

Gupta, Aayushi. "Are You Stuck in the Vicious Cycle of Overthinking? It's Risky, Warns an Expert." Healthshots, 29 Apr. 2022, www.healthshots.com/mind/mental-health/heres-how-overthinking-can-impact-your-overall-health/.

"How to Let Go of Anger: Seneca's 16 Stoic Techniques." HighExistence | Explore Life's Deepest Questions, 8 June 2018, www.highexistence.com/seneca-on-how-to-deal-with-anger/. Accessed 6 Apr. 2024.

Lake, Tim. "An In-Depth Understanding on the Four Virtues of Stoicism." TheCollector, 20 Dec. 2022, www.thecollector.com/four-cardinal-virtues-stoicism/.

partners, UV Content. "7 Benefits of Being in the Now." UV Consultants, 3 Dec. 2020, www.uvconsultants.com/post/7-benefits-of-being-in-the-now. Accessed 6 Apr. 2024.

Suraliya, Sonia. "11 Reasons Why Kindness Is Important." Your Mental Health Pal, 22 Mar. 2022, yourmentalhealthpal.com/importance-of-kindness/.

"The Discourses Summary PDF | Epictetus." The Discourses Summary PDF | Epictetus, www.bookey.app/book/the-discourses. Accessed 6 Apr. 2024.

"The Life of Seneca | Psychology Today." Www.psychologytoday.com, www.psychologytoday.com/us/blog/ataraxia/202311/the-life-of-seneca. Accessed 6 Apr. 2024.

"What Are the Origins of Stoicism?" TheCollector, 1 July 2022, www.thecollector.com/what-are-the-origins-of-stoicism-history. Accessed 6 Apr. 2024.

"What Are the Origins of Stoicism?" TheCollector, 1 July 2022, www.thecollector.com/what-are-the-origins-of-stoicism-history. Accessed 6 Apr. 2024.